The Ruin of Britain

St. Gildas the Wise

Translated by: Thomas Habington,
John Allen Giles

Dalcassian
Publishing
Company
PHILADELPHIA, PA

Library of Congress Cataloging-in-Publication Data

Copyright © 2018 Dalcassian Publishing Co.
In association with St. Macartan Press
All rights reserved.

I. THE PREFACE

1

Whatever in this my epistle I may write in my humble but well-meaning manner, rather by way of lamentation than for display, let no one suppose that it springs from contempt of others or that I foolishly esteem myself as better than they;—for alas! the subject of my complaint is the general destruction of every thing that is good, and the general growth of evil throughout the land;—but that I rejoice to see her revive therefrom: for it is my present purpose to relate the deeds of an indolent and slothful race, rather than the exploits of those who have been valiant in the field.[1] I have kept silence, I confess, with much mental anguish, compunction of feeling and contrition of heart, whilst I revolved all these things within myself; and, as God the searcher of the reins is witness, for the space of even ten years or more, [my inexperience, as at present also, and my unworthiness preventing me from taking upon myself the character of a censor. But I read how the illustrious lawgiver, for one word's doubting, was not allowed to enter the desired land; that the sons of the high-priest, for placing strange fire upon God's altar, were cut off by a speedy death; that God's people, for breaking the law of God, save two only, were slain by wild beasts, by fire and sword in the deserts of Arabia, though God had so loved them that he had made a way for them through the Red Sea, had fed them with bread from heaven, and water from the rock, and by the lifting up of a hand merely had made their armies invincible; and then, when they had crossed the Jordan and entered the unknown land, and the walls of the city had fallen down flat at the sound only of a trumpet, the taking of a cloak and a little gold from the accursed things caused the deaths of many: and again the breach of their treaty with the Gibeonites, though that treaty had been obtained by fraud, brought destruction upon many; and I took warning from the sins of the people which called down upon them the reprehensions of the prophets and also of Jeremiah, with his fourfold Lamentations written in alphabetical order. I saw moreover in my own time, as that prophet also had complained, that the city had sat down lone and widowed, which before was full of people; that the queen of nations and the princess of provinces (i.e. the church), had been made tributary; that the gold was obscured, and the most excellent colour (which is the brightness of God's word) changed; that the sons of Sion (i.e. of holy mother church), once famous and clothed in the finest gold, grovelled in dung; and what added intolerably to the weight of grief of that illustrious man, and to mine, though but an abject, whilst he had thus mourned them in their happy and prosperous condition, "Her Nazarites were fairer than snow, more ruddy than old ivory, more beautiful than the saphire." These and many other passages in the ancient Scriptures I regarded as a kind of mirror of human life, and I turned also to the New, wherein I read more clearly what perhaps to me before was dark, for the darkness fled, and truth shed her steady light-I read therein that the Lord had said, "I came not but to the lost sheep of the house of Israel;" and on the other hand, "But the children of this kingdom shall be cast out into outer darkness; there shall be weeping and gnashing of teeth:" and again, "It is not good to take the children's meat and to give it to dogs:" also, "Woe to you, scribes and pharisees, hypocrites!" I heard how "many shall come from the east and the west and shall sit down with Abraham, Isaac, and Jacob in the kingdom of heaven:" and on the contrary, "I will then say to them 'Depart from me, ye workers of iniquity!'" I read, "Blessed are the barren and the teats which have not given suck;" and on the contrary, "Those, who were ready, entered with him to the wedding; afterwards came the other virgins also, saying 'Lord, Lord, open to us:' to whom it was answered, 'I do not know you.'" I heard, forsooth, "Whoever shall believe and be baptized, shall be saved, but whoever shall not believe shall be damned." I read in the words of the apostle that the branch of the wild olive was grafted upon the good olive, but should nevertheless be cut off from the communion of the root of its fatness, if it did not hold itself in fear, but entertained lofty thoughts. I knew the mercy of the Lord, but I also feared his judgment: I praised his grace, but I feared the rendering to every man according to his works: perceiving the sheep of the same fold to be different, I deservedly commended Peter for his entire confession of Christ, but called Judas most wretched, for his love of covetousness: I thought Stephen most glorious on account of the palm of martyrdom, but Nicholas wretched for his mark of unclean heresy: I read assuredly, "They had all things common:" but likewise also, as it is written, "Why have ye conspired to tempt the Spirit of God?" I saw, on the other hand, how much security had grown upon the men of our time, as if there were nothing to cause them fear. These things, therefore, and many more which for brevity's sake we have determined to omit, I revolved again and again in my amazed mind with compunction in my heart, and I thought to myself, "If God's peculiar people, chosen from all the people of the world, the royal seed, and holy nation, to whom he had said, 'My first begotten Israel,' its priests, prophets, and kings, throughout so many ages, his servant and apostle, and the members of his primitive church, were not spared when the deviated from the right path, what will he do to the darkness of this our age, in which, besides all the huge and heinous sins, which it has common with all the wicked of the world committed, is found an innate, indelible, and irremediable load of folly and inconstancy?" "What, wretched man (I say to myself) is it given to you, as if you were an illustrious and learned teacher, to oppose the force of so violent a torrent, and keep the charge committed to you against such a series of inveterate crimes which has spread far and wide, without interruption, for so many years? Hold thy peace: to do otherwise, is to tell the foot to see, and the hand to speak. Britain has rulers, and she has watchmen: why dost thou incline thyself thus uselessly to prate?" She has such, I say, not too many, perhaps, but surely not too few: but, because they are bent down and pressed beneath so heavy a burden, they have not time allowed them to take breath. My senses, therefore, as if feeling a portion of my debt and obligation, preoccupied themselves with such objections, and with others yet more strong. They struggled, as I said, no short time, in fearful strait, whilst I read, "There is a time for speaking, and a time for keeping silence." At length, the creditor's side prevailed and bore off the victory: if (said he) thou art not bold enough to be marked with the comely mark of golden liberty among the prophetic creatures, who enjoy the rank as reasoning beings next to the angels, refuse not the inspiration of the understanding ass, to that day dumb, which would not carry forward the tiara'd magician who was going to curse God's people, but in the narrow pass of the vineyard crushed his loosened foot, and thereby felt the lash; and though he was, with his ungrateful and furious hand, against right justice, beating her innocent sides, she pointed out to him the heavenly messenger holding the naked sword, and standing in his way, though he had not seen him.]

Wherefore in zeal for the house of God and for his holy law, constrained either by the reasonings of my own thoughts, or by the pious entreaties of my brethren, I now discharge the debt so long exacted of me; humble, indeed, in style, but faithful, as I think, and friendly to all Christ's youthful soldiers, but severe and insupportable to foolish apostates; the former of whom, if I am not deceived, will receive the same with tears flowing from god's love; but the others with sorrow, such as is extorted from the indignation and pusillanimity of a convicted conscience.

2

I will, therefore, if God be willing, endeavour to say a few words about the situation of Britain, her disobedience and subjection, her rebellion, second subjection and dreadful slavery—of her religion, persecution, holy martyrs, heresies of different kinds—of her tyrants, her two hostile and ravaging nations—of her first devastation, her defence, her second devastation, and second taking vengeance—of her third devastation, of her famine, and the letters to Agitius[2]—of her victory and her crimes—of the sudden rumour of enemies—of her famous pestilence—of her counsels—of her last enemy, far more cruel than the first—of the subversion of her cities, and of the remnant that escaped; and finally, of the peace which, by the will of God, has been granted her in these our times.

II. THE HISTORY

3

The island of Britain, situated on almost the utmost border of the earth, towards the south and west, and poised in the divine balance, as it is said, which supports the whole world, stretches out from the south-west towards the north pole, and is eight hundred miles long and two hundred broad,[3] except where the headlands of sundry promontories stretch farther into the sea. It is surrounded by the ocean, which forms winding bays, and is strongly defended by this ample, and, if I may so call it, impassable barrier, save on the south side, where the narrow sea affords a passage to Belgic Gaul. It is enriched by the mouths of two noble rivers, the Thames and the Severn, as it were two arms, by which foreign luxuries were of old imported, and by other streams of less importance. It is famous for eight and twenty cities, and is embellished by certain castles, with walls, towers, well barred gates, and houses with threatening battlements built on high, and provided with all requisite instruments of defence. Its plains are spacious, its hills are pleasantly situated, adapted for superior tillage, and its mountains are admirably calculated for the alternate pasturage of cattle, where flowers of various colours, trodden by the feet of man, give it the appearance of a lovely picture. It is decked, like a man's chosen bride, with divers jewels, with lucid fountains and abundant brooks wandering over the snow white sands; with transparent rivers, flowing in gentle murmurs, and offering a sweet pledge of slumber[4] to those who recline upon their banks, whilst it is irrigated by abundant lakes, which pour forth cool torrents of refreshing water.

4

This island, stiff-necked and stubborn-minded, from the time of its being first inhabited, ungratefully rebels, sometimes against God, sometimes against her own citizens, and frequently also, against foreign kings and their subjects. For what can there either be, or be committed, more disgraceful or more unrighteous in human affairs, than to refuse to show fear to God or affection to one's own countrymen, and (without detriment to one's faith) to refuse due honour to those of higher dignity, to cast off all regard to reason, human and divine, and, in contempt of heaven and earth, to be guided by one's own sensual inventions? I shall, therefore, omit those ancient errors common to all the nations of the earth, in which, before Christ came in the flesh, all mankind were bound; nor shall I enumerate those diabolical idols of my country, which almost surpassed in number those of Egypt, and of which we still see some mouldering away within or without the deserted temples, with stiff and deformed features as was customary. Nor will I call out upon the mountains, fountains, or hills, or upon the rivers, which now are subservient to the use of men, but once were an abomination and destruction to them, and to which the blind people paid divine honour. I shall also pass over the bygone times of our cruel tyrants, whose notoriety was spread over to far distant countries; so that Porphyry, that dog who in the east was always so fierce against the church, in his mad and vain style added this also, that "Britain is a land fertile in tyrants."[5] I will only endeavour to relate the evils which Britain suffered in the times of the Roman emperors, and also those which she caused to distant states; but so far as lies in my power, I shall not follow the writings and records of my own country, which (if there ever were any of them) have been consumed in the fires of the enemy, or have accompanied my exiled countrymen into distant lands, but be guided by the relations of foreign writers, which, being broken and interrupted in many places are therefore by no means clear.

5

For when the rulers of Rome had obtained the empire of the world, subdued all the neighbouring nations and islands towards the east, and strengthened their renown by the first peace which they made with the Parthians, who border on India, there was a general cessation from war throughout the whole world; the fierce flame which they kindled could not be extinguished or checked by the Western Ocean, but passing beyond the sea, imposed submission upon our island without resistance, and entirely reduced to obedience its unwarlike but faithless people, not so much by fire and sword and warlike engines, like other nations, but threats alone, and menaces of judgments frowning on their countenance, whilst terror penetrated to their hearts.

6

When afterwards they returned to Rome, for want of pay, as is said, and had no suspicion of an approaching rebellion, that deceitful lioness[6] put to death the rulers who had been left among them, to unfold more fully and to confirm the enterprises of the Romans. When the report of these things reached the senate, and they with a speedy army made haste to take vengeance on the crafty foxes,[7] as they called them, there was no bold navy on the sea to fight bravely for the country; by land there was no marshalled army, no right wing of battle, nor other preparation for resistance; but their backs were their shields against their vanquishers, and they presented their necks to their swords, whilst chill terror ran through every limb, and they stretched out their hands to be bound, like women; so that it has become a proverb far and wide, that the Britons are neither brave in war nor faithful in time of peace.

7

The Romans, therefore, having slain many of the rebels, and reserved others for slaves, that the land might not be entirely reduced to desolation, left the island, destitute as it was of wine and oil, and returned to Italy, leaving behind them taskmasters, to scourge the shoulders of the natives, to reduce their necks to the yoke, and their soil to the vassalage of a Roman province; to chastise the crafty race, not with warlike weapons, but with rods, and if necessary to gird upon their sides the naked sword, so that it was no longer thought to be Britain, but a Roman island; and all their money, whether of copper, gold, or silver, was stamped with Caesar's image.

8

Meanwhile these islands, stiff with cold and frost, and in a distant region of the world, remote from the visible sun, received the beams of light, that is, the holy precepts of Christ, the true Sun, showing to the whole world his splendour, not only from the temporal firmament, but from the height of heaven, which surpasses every thing temporal, at the latter part, as we know, of the reign of Tiberius Caesar, by whom his religion was propagated without impediment, and death threatened to those who interfered with its professors.

9

These rays of light were received with lukewarm minds by the inhabitants, but they nevertheless took root among some of them in a greater or less degree, until the nine years' persecution of the tyrant Diocletian, when the churches throughout the whole world were overthrown, all the copies of the Holy Scriptures which could be found burned in the streets, and the chosen pastors of God's flock butchered, together with their innocent sheep, in order that not a vestige, if possible, might remain in some provinces of Christ's religion. What disgraceful flights then took place-what slaughter and death inflicted by way of punishment in divers shapes,—what dreadful apostacies from religion; and on the contrary, what glorious crowns of martyrdom then were won,— what raving fury was displayed by the persecutors, and patience on the part of the suffering saints, ecclesiastical history informs us; for the whole church were crowding in a body, to leave behind them the dark things of this world, and to make the best of their way to the happy mansions of heaven, as if to their proper home.

10

God, therefore, who wishes all men to be saved, and who calls sinners no less than those who think themselves righteous, magnified his mercy towards us, and, as we know, during the above-named persecution, that Britain might not totally be enveloped in the dark shades of night, he, of his own free gift, kindled up among us bright luminaries of holy martyrs, whose places of burial and of martyrdom, had they not for our manifold crimes been interfered with and destroyed by the barbarians, would have still kindled in the minds of the beholders no small fire of divine charity. Such were St. Alban of Verulam, Aaron and Julius, citizens of Carlisle,[8] and the rest, of both sexes, who in different places stood their ground in the Christian contest.

11

The first of these martyrs, St. Alban, for charity's sake saved another confessor who was pursued by his persecutors, and was on the point of being seized, by hiding him in his house, and then by changing clothes with him, imitating in this example of Christ, who laid down his life for his sheep, and exposing himself in the other's clothes to be pursued in his stead. So pleasing to God was this conduct, that between his confession and martyrdom, he was honoured with the performance of wonderful miracles in presence of the impious blasphemers who were carrying the Roman standards, and like the Israelites of old, who trod dry-foot an unfrequented path whilst the ark of the covenant stood some time on the sands in the midst of Jordan; so also the martyr, with a thousand others, opened a path across the noble river Thames, whose waters stood abrupt like precipices on either side; and seeing this, the first of his executors was stricken with awe, and from a wolf became a lamb; so that he thirsted for martyrdom, and boldly underwent that for which he thirsted. The other holy martyrs were tormented with divers sufferings, and their limbs were racked in such unheard of ways, that they, without delay, erected the trophies of their glorious martyrdom even in the gates of the city of Jerusalem. For those who survived, hid themselves in woods and deserts, and secret caves, waiting until God, who is the righteous judge of all, should reward their persecutors with judgment, and themselves with protection of their lives.

12

In less than ten years, therefore, of the above-named persecution, and when these bloody decrees began to fail in consequence of the death of their authors, all Christ's young disciples, after so long and wintry a night, begin to behold the genial light of heaven. They rebuild the churches, which had been levelled to the ground; they found, erect, and finish churches to the holy martyrs, and everywhere show their ensigns as token of their victory; festivals are celebrated and sacraments received with clean hearts and lips, and all the church's sons rejoice as it were in the fostering bosom of a mother. For this holy union remained between Christ their head and the members of his church, until the Arian treason, fatal as a serpent, and vomiting its poison from beyond the sea, caused deadly dissension between brothers inhabiting the same house, and thus, as if a road were made across the sea, like wild beasts of all descriptions, and darting the poison of every heresy from their jaws, they inflicted dreadful wounds upon their country, which is ever desirous to hear something new, and remains constant long to nothing.

13

At length also, new races of tyrants sprang up, in terrific numbers, and the island, still bearing its Roman name, but casting off her institutes and laws, sent forth among the Gauls that bitter scion of her own planting Maximus, with a great number of followers, and the ensigns of royalty, which he bore without decency and without lawful right, but in a tyrannical manner, and amid the disturbances of the seditious soldiery. He, by cunning arts rather than by valour, attaching to his rule, by perjury and falsehood, all the neighbouring towns and provinces, against the Roman state, extended one of his wings to Spain, the other to Italy, fixed the seat of his unholy government at Treves, and so furiously pushed his rebellion against his lawful emperors that he drove one of them out of Rome, and caused the other to terminate his most holy life. Trusting to these successful attempts, he not long after lost his accursed head before the walls of Aquileia, whereas he had before cut off the crowned heads of almost all the world.

14

After this, Britain is left deprived of all her soldiery and armed bands, of her cruel governors, and of the flower of her youth, who went with Maximus, but never again returned; and utterly ignorant as she was of the art of war, groaned in amazement for many years under the cruelty of two foreign nations—the Scots from the north-west, and the Picts from the north.

15

The Britons, impatient at the assaults of the Scots and Picts, their hostilities and dreadful oppressions, send ambassadors to Rome with letters, entreating in piteous terms the assistance of an armed band to protect them, and offering loyal and ready submission to the authority of Rome, if they only would expel their foes. A legion is immediately sent, forgetting their past rebellion, and provided sufficiently with arms. When they had crossed over the sea and landed, they came at once to close conflict with their cruel enemies, and slew great numbers of them. All of them were driven beyond the borders, and the humiliated natives rescued from the bloody slavery which awaited them. By the advice of their protectors, they now built a wall across the island from one sea to the other, which being manned with a proper force, might be a terror to the foes whom it was intended to repel, and a protection to their friends whom it covered. But this wall, being made of turf instead of stone, was of no use to that foolish people, who had no head to guide them.

16

The Roman legion had no sooner returned home in joy and triumph, than their former foes, like hungry and ravening wolves, rushing with greedy jaws upon the fold which is left without a shepherd, and wafted both by the strength of oarsmen and the blowing wind, break through the boundaries, and spread slaughter on every side, and like mowers cutting down the ripe corn, they cut up, tread under foot, and overrun the whole country.

17

And now again they send suppliant ambassadors, with their garments rent and their heads covered with ashes, imploring assistance from the Romans, and like timorous chickens, crowding under the protecting wings of their parents, that their wretched country might not altogether be destroyed, and that the Roman name, which now was but an empty sound to fill the ear, might not become a reproach even to distant nations. Upon this, the Romans, moved with compassion, as far as human nature can be, at the relations of such horrors, send forward, like eagles in their flight, their unexpected bands of cavalry by land and mariners by sea, and planting their terrible swords upon the shoulders of their enemies, they mow them down like leaves which fall at the destined period; and as a mountain-torrent swelled with numerous streams, and bursting its banks with roaring noise, with foaming crest and yeasty wave rising to the stars, by whose eddying currents our eyes are as it were dazzled, does with one of its billows overwhelm every obstacle in its way, so did our illustrious defenders vigorously drive our enemies' band beyond the sea, if any could so escape them; for it was beyond those same seas that they transported, year after year, the plunder which they had gained, no one daring to resist them.

18

The Romans, therefore, left the country, giving notice that they could no longer be harassed by such laborious expeditions, nor suffer the Roman standards, with so large and brave an army, to be worn out by sea and land by fighting against these unwarlike, plundering vagabonds; but that the islanders, inuring themselves to warlike weapons, and bravely fighting, should valiantly protect their country, their property, wives and children, and, what is dearer than these, their liberty and lives; that they should not suffer their hands to be tied behind their backs by a nation which, unless they were enervated by idleness and sloth, was not more powerful than themselves, but that they should arm those hands with buckler, sword, and spear, ready for the field of battle; and, because they thought this also of advantage to the people they were about to leave, they, with the help of the miserable natives, built a wall different from the former, by public and private contributions, and of the same structure as walls generally, extending in a straight line from sea to sea, between some cities, which, from fear of their enemies, had there by chance been built. They then give energetic counsel to the timorous natives, and leave them patterns by which to manufacture arms. Moreover, on the south coast where their vessels lay, as there was some apprehension lest the barbarians might land, they erected towers at stated intervals, commanding a prospect of the sea; and then left the island never to return.

19

No sooner were they gone, than the Picts and Scots, like worms which in the heat of the mid-day come forth from their holes, hastily land again from their canoes, in which they had been carried beyond the Cichican[2] valley, differing one from another in manners, but inspired with the same avidity for blood, and all more eager to shroud their villainous faces in bushy hair than to cover with decent clothing those parts of their body which required it. Moreover, having heard of the departure of our friends, and their resolution never to return, they seized with greater boldness than before on all the country towards the extreme north as far as the wall. To oppose them there was placed on the heights a garrison equally slow to fight and ill adapted to run away, a useless and panic-struck company, who slumbered away days and nights on their unprofitable watch. Meanwhile the hooked weapons of their enemies were not idle, and our wretched countrymen were dragged from the wall and dashed against the ground. Such premature death, however, painful as it was, saved them from seeing the miserable sufferings of their brothers and children. But why should I say more? They left their cities, abandoned the protection of the wall, and dispersed themselves in flight more desperately than before. The enemy, on the other hand, pursued them with more unrelenting cruelty than before, and butchered our countrymen like sheep, so that their habitations were like those of savage beasts; for they turned their arms upon each other, and for the sake of a little sustenance, imbrued their hands in the blood of their fellow countrymen. Thus foreign calamities were augmented by domestic feuds; so that the whole country was entirely destitute of provisions, save such as could be procured in the chase.

20

Again, therefore, the wretched remnant, sending to Aetius, a powerful Roman citizen, address him as follow:—"To Aetius,[10] now consul for the third time: the groans of the Britons." And again a little further, thus:—"The barbarians drive us to the sea; the sea throws us back on the barbarians: thus two modes of death await us, we are either slain or drowned." The Romans, however, could not assist them, and in the meantime the discomfited people, wandering in the woods, began to feel the effects of a severe famine, which compelled many of them without delay to yield themselves up to their cruel persecutors, to obtain subsistence: others of them, however, lying hid in mountains, caves and woods, continually sallied out from thence to renew the war. And then it was, for the first time, that they overthrew their enemies, who had for so many years been living in their country; for their trust was not in man, but in God; according to the maxim of Philo, "We must have divine assistance, when that of man fails." The boldness of the enemy was for a while checked, but not the wickedness of our countrymen; the enemy left our people, but the people did not leave their sins.

21

For it has always been a custom with our nation, as it is at present, to be impotent in repelling foreign foes, but bold and invincible in raising civil war, and bearing the burdens of their offences: they are impotent, I say, in following the standard of peace and truth, but bold in wickedness and falsehood. The audacious invaders therefore return to their winter quarters, determined before long again to return and plunder. And then, too, the Picts for the first time seated themselves at the extremity of the island, where they afterwards continued, occasionally plundering and wasting the country. During these truces, the wounds of the distressed people are healed, but another sore, still more venomous, broke out. No sooner were the ravages of the enemy checked, than the island was deluged with a most extraordinary plenty of all things, greater than was before known, and with it grew up every kind of luxury and licentiousness. It grew with so firm a root, that one might truly say of it, "Such fornication is heard of among you, as never was known the like among the Gentiles." But besides this vice, there arose also every other, to which human nature is liable and in particular that hatred of truth, together with her supporters, which still at present destroys every thing good in the island; the love of falsehood, together with its inventors, the reception of crime in the place of virtue, the respect shown to wickedness rather than goodness, the love of darkness instead of the sun, the admission of Satan as an angel of light. Kings were anointed, not according to god's ordinance, but such as showed themselves more cruel than the rest; and soon after, they were put to death by those who had elected them, without any inquiry into their merits, but because others still more cruel were chosen to succeed them. If any one of these was of a milder nature than the rest, or in any way more regardful of the truth, he was looked upon as the ruiner of the country, every body cast a dart at him, and they valued things alike whether pleasing or displeasing to God, unless it so happened that what displeased him was pleasing to themselves. So that the words of the prophet, addressed to the people of old, might well be applied to our own countrymen: "Children without a law, have ye left God and provoked to anger the holy one of Israel?[111] Why will ye still inquire, adding iniquity? Every head is languid and every heart is sad; from the sole of the foot to the crown, there is no health in him." And thus they did all things contrary to their salvation, as if no remedy could be applied to the world by the true Physician of all men. And not only the laity did so, but our Lord's own flock and its shepherds, who ought to have been an example to the people, slumbered away their time in drunkenness, as if they had been dipped in wine; whilst the swellings of pride, the jar of strife, the griping talons of envy, and the confused estimate of right and wrong, got such entire possession of the, that there seemed to be poured out (and the same still continueth) contempt upon princes, and to be made by their vanities to wander astray and not in the way.

22

Meanwhile, God being willing to purify his family who were infected by so deep a stain of woe, and at the hearing only of their calamities to amend them; a vague rumour suddenly as if on wings reaches the ears of all, that their inveterate foes were rapidly approaching to destroy the whole country, and to take possession of it, as of old, from one end to the other. But yet they derived no advantage from this intelligence; for, like frantic beasts, taking the bit of reason between their teeth, they abandoned the safe and narrow road, and rushed forward upon the broad downward path of vice, which leads to death. Whilst, therefore, as Solomon says, the stubborn servant is not cured by words, the fool is scourged and feels it not: a pestilential disease morally affected the foolish people, which, without the sword, cut off so large a number of persons, that the living were not able to bury them. But even this was no warning to them, that in them also might be fulfilled the words of Isaiah the prophet, "And God hath called his people to lamentation, to baldness, and to the girdle of sackcloth; behold they begin to kill calves, and to slay rams, to eat, to drink, and to say, 'We will eat and drink, for to-morrow we shall die.'" For the time was approaching, when all their iniquities, as formerly those of the Amorrhaeans, should be fulfilled. For a council was called to settle what was best and most expedient to be done, in order to repel such frequent and fatal irruptions and plunderings of the above-named nations.

23

Then all the councillors, together with that proud tyrant Gurthrigern [Vortigern], the British king, were so blinded, that, as a protection to their country, they sealed its doom by inviting in among them like wolves into the sheep-fold), the fierce and impious Saxons, a race hateful both to God and men, to repel the invasions of the northern nations. Nothing was ever so pernicious to our country, nothing was ever so unlucky. What palpable darkness must have enveloped their minds-darkness desperate and cruel! Those very people whom, when absent, they dreaded more than death itself, were invited to reside, as one may say, under the selfsame roof. Foolish are the princes, as it is said, of Thafneos, giving counsel to unwise Pharaoh. A multitude of whelps came forth from the lair of this barbaric lioness, in three *cyuls*, as they call them, that is, in their ships of war, with their sails wafted by the wind and with omens and prophecies favourable, for it was foretold by a certain soothsayer among them, that they should occupy the country to which they were sailing three hundred years, and half of that time, a hundred and fifty years, should plunder and despoil the same. They first landed on the eastern side of the island, by the invitation of the unlucky king, and there fixed their sharp talons, apparently to fight in favour of the island, but alas! more truly against it. Their mother-land, finding her first brood thus successful, sends forth a larger company of her wolfish offspring, which sailing over, join themselves to their bastard-born comrades. From that time the germ of iniquity and the root of contention planted their poison amongst us, as we deserved, and shot forth into leaves and branches. the barbarians being thus introduced as soldiers into the island, to encounter, as they falsely said, any dangers in defence of their hospitable entertainers, obtain an allowance of provisions, which, for some time being plentifully bestowed, stopped their doggish mouths. Yet they complain that their monthly supplies are not furnished in sufficient abundance, and they industriously aggravate each occasion of quarrel, saying that unless more liberality is shown them, they will break the treaty and plunder the whole island. In a short time, they follow up their threats with deeds.

24

For the fire of vengeance, justly kindled by former crimes, spread from sea to sea, fed by the hands of our foes in the east, and did not cease, until, destroying the neighbouring towns and lands, it reached the other side of the island, and dipped its red and savage tongue in the western ocean. In these assaults, therefore, not unlike that of the Assyrian upon Judea, was fulfilled in our case what the prophet describes in words of lamentation; "They have burned with fire the sanctuary; they have polluted on earth the tabernacle of thy name." And again, "O God, the gentiles have come into thine inheritance;

thy holy temple have they defiled," &c. So that all the columns were levelled with the ground by the frequent strokes of the battering-ram, all the husbandmen routed, together with their bishops, priests, and people, whilst the sword gleamed, and the flames crackled around them on every side. Lamentable to behold, in the midst of the streets lay the tops of lofty towers, tumbled to the ground, stones of high walls, holy altars, fragments of human bodies, covered with livid clots of coagulated blood, looking as if they had been squeezed together in a press;* and with no chance of being buried, save in the ruins of the houses, or in the ravening bellies of wild beasts and birds; with reverence be it spoken for their blessed souls, if, indeed, there were many found who were carried, at that time, into the high heaven by the holy angels. So entirely had the vintage, once so fine, degenerated and become bitter, that, in the words of the prophet, there was hardly a grape or ear of corn to be seen where the husbandman had turned his back.

25

Some therefore, of the miserable remnant, being taken in the mountains, were murdered in great numbers; others, constrained by famine, came and yielded themselves to be slaves for ever to their foes, running the risk of being instantly slain, which truly was the greatest favour that could be offered them: some others passed beyond the seas with loud lamentations instead of the voice of exhortation. "Thou hast given us as sheep to be slaughtered, and among the Gentiles hast thou dispersed us." Others, committing the safeguard of their lives, which were in continual jeopardy, to the mountains, precipices, thickly wooded forests, and to the rocks of the seas (albeit with trembling hearts), remained still in their country. But in the meanwhile, an opportunity happening, when these most cruel robbers were returned home, the poor remnants of our nation (to whom flocked from divers places round about our miserable countrymen as fast as bees to their hives, for fear of an ensuing storm), being strengthened by God, calling upon him with all their hearts, as the poet says,—"With their unnumbered vows they burden heaven," that they might not be brought to utter destruction, took arms under the conduct of Ambrosius Aurelianus, a modest man, who of all the Roman nation was then alone in the confusion of this troubled period by chance left alive. His parents, who for their merit were adorned with the purple, had been slain in these same broils, and now his progeny in these our days, although shamefully degenerated from the worthiness of their ancestors, provoke to battle their cruel conquerors, and by the goodness of our Lord obtain the victory.

26

After this, sometimes our countrymen, sometimes the enemy, won the field, to the end that our Lord might in this land try after his accustomed manner these his Israelites, whether they loved him or not, until the year of the siege of Bath-hill, when took place also the last almost, though not the least slaughter of our cruel foes, which was (as I am sure) forty-four years and one month after the landing of the Saxons, and also the time of my own nativity. And yet neither to this day are the cities of our country inhabited as before, but being forsaken and overthrown, still lie desolate; our foreign wars having ceased, but our civil troubles still remaining. For as well the remembrance of such terrible desolation of the island, as also of the unexpected recovery of the same, remained in the minds of those who were eyewitnesses of the wonderful events of both, and in regard thereof, kings, public magistrates, and private persons, with priests and clergymen, did all and every one of them live orderly according to their several vocations. But when these had departed out of this world, and a new race succeeded, who were ignorant of this troublesome time, and had only experience of the present prosperity, all the laws of truth and justice were so shaken and subverted, that not so much as a vestige or remembrance of these virtues remained among the above-named orders of men, except among a very few who, compared with the great multitude which were daily rushing headlong down to hell, are accounted so small a number, that our reverend mother, the church, scarcely beholds them, her only true children, reposing in her bosom; whose worthy lives, being a pattern to all men, and beloved of God, inasmuch as by their holy prayers, as by certain pillars and most profitable supporters, our infirmity is sustained up, that it may not utterly be broken down, I would have no one suppose I intended to reprove, if forced by the increasing multitude of offences, I have freely, aye, with anguish, not so much declared as bewailed the wickedness of those who are become servants, not only to their bellies, but also to the devil rather than to Christ, who is our blessed God, world without end.

For why shall their countrymen conceal what foreign nations round about now not only know, but also continually are casting in their teeth?

III. THE EPISTLE

27

Britain has kings, but they are tyrants; she has judges, but unrighteous ones; generally engaged in plunder and rapine, but always preying on the innocent; whenever they exert themselves to avenge or protect, it is sure to be in favour of robbers and criminals; they have an abundance of wives, yet are they addicted to fornication and adultery; they are ever ready to take oaths, and as often perjure themselves; they make a vow and almost immediately act falsely; they make war, but their wars are against their countrymen, and are unjust ones; they rigorously prosecute thieves throughout their country, but those who sit at table with them are robbers, and they not only cherish but reward them; they give alms plentifully, but in contrast to this is a whole pile of crimes which they have committed; they sit on the seat of justice, but rarely seek for the rule of right judgment; they despise the innocent and the humble, but seize every occasion of exalting to the utmost the bloody-minded; the proud, murderers, the combined and adulterers, enemies of God, who ought to be utterly destroyed and their names forgotten.

They have many prisoners in their gaols, loaded with chains, but this is done in treachery rather than in just punishment for crimes; and when they have stood before the altar, swearing by the name of God, they go away and think no more of the holy altar than if it were a mere heap of dirty stones.

28

this horrid abomination, Constantine, the tyrannical whelp of the unclean lioness of Damnonia, is not ignorant.

This same year, after taking a dreadful oath (whereby he bound himself first before God, by a solemn protestation, and then called all the saints, and Mother of God, to witness, that he would not contrive any deceit against his countrymen), he nevertheless, in the habit of a holy abbat amid the sacred altars, did with sword and javelin, as if with teeth, wound and tear, even in the bosoms of their temporal mother, and of the church their spiritual mother, two royal youths, with their two attendants, whose arms, although not eased in armour, were yet boldly used, and, stretched out towards God and his altar, will hang up at the gates of thy city, O Christ, the venerable ensigns of their faith and patience; and when he had done it, the cloaks, red with coagulated blood, did touch the place of the heavenly sacrifice. And not one worthy act could he boast of previous to this cruel deed; for many years before he had stained himself with the abomination of many adulteries, having put away his wife contrary to the command of Christ, the teacher of the world, who hath said: "What God hath joined together, let not man separate," and again: "Husbands, love your wives." For he had planted in the ground of his heart (an unfruitful soil for any good seed) a bitter scion of incredulity and folly, taken from the vine of Sodom, which being watered with his vulgar and domestic impieties, like poisonous showers, and afterwards audaciously springing up to the offence of God, brought forth into the world the sin of horrible murder and sacrilege; and not yet discharged from the entangling nets of his former offences, he added new wickedness to the former.

29

Go to now, I reprove thee as present, whom I know as yet to be in this life extant. Why standest thou astonished, O thou butcher of thine own soul? Why cost thou wilfully kindle against thyself the eternal fires of hell? Why cost thou, in place of enemies, desperately stab thyself with shine own sword, with shine own javelin? Cannot those same poisonous cups of offences yet satisfy thy stomach? I look back (I beseech thee) and come to Christ (for thou labourest, and art pressed down to the earth with this huge burden), and he himself, as he said, will give thee rest. Come to him who wisheth not the death of a sinner, but that he should be rather converted and live. Unloose (according to the prophet) the bands of thy neck, O thou son of Sion. Return (I pray thee), although from the far remote regions of sins, unto the most holy Father, who, for his son that will despise the filthy food of swine, and fear a death of cruel famine, and so come back to him again, hath with great joy been accustomed to kill his fatted calf, and bring forth for the wanderer, the first robe and royal ring, and then taking as it were a taste of the heavenly hope, thou shalt perceive how sweet our Lord is. For if thou cost contemn these, be thou assured, thou shalt almost instantly be tossed and tormented in the inevitable and dark floods of endless fire.

30

What cost thou also, thou lion's whelp (as the prophet saith), Aurelius Conanus? Art not thou as the former (if not far more foul) to thy utter destruction, swallowed up in the filthiness of horrible murders, fornications, and adulteries, as by an overwhelming flood of the sea? Hast not thou by hating, as a deadly serpent, the peace of thy country, and thirsting unjustly after civil wars and frequent spoil, shut the gates of heavenly peace and repose against thine own soul? Being now left alone as a withering tree in the midst of a field, remember (I beseech thee) the vain and idle fancies of thy parents and brethren, together with the untimely death that befell them in the prime of their youth; and shalt thou, for thy religious deserts, be reserved out of all thy family to live a hundred years, or to attain to the age of a Methusalem? No, surely, but unless (as the psalmist saith) thou shalt be speedily converted unto our Lord, that King will shortly brandish his sword against thee, who hath said by his prophet, "I will kill, and I will cause to live; I will strike, and I will heal; and there is no one who can deliver out of my hand." Be thou therefore shaken out of thy filthy dust, and with all thy heart converted to Him who hath created thee, that "when his wrath shall shortly burn out, thou mayst be blessed by fixing thy hopes on him." But if otherwise, eternal pains will be heaped up for thee, where thou shalt be ever tormented and never consumed in the cruel jaws of hell.

31

Thou also, who like to the spotted leopard, art diverse in manners and in mischief, whose head now is growing grey, who art seated on a throne full of deceits, and from the bottom even to the top art stained with murder and adulteries, thou naughty son of a good king, like Manasses sprung from Ezechiah, Vortipore, thou foolish tyrant of the Demetians, why art thou so stiff? What! do not such violent gulfs of sin (which thou dost swallow up like pleasant wine, nay rather which swallow thee up), as yet satisfy thee, especially since the end of thy life is daily now approaching? Why cost thou heavily clog thy miserable soul with the sin of lust, which is fouler than any other, by putting away thy wife, and after her honourable death, by the base practices of thy shameless daughter? Waste not (I beseech thee) the residue of thy life in offending God, because as yet an acceptable time and day of salvation shines on the faces of the penitent, wherein thou mayest take care that thy flight may not be in the winter, or on the sabbath day. "Turn away (according to the psalmist) from evil, and do good, seek peace and ensue it," because the eyes of our Lord will be cast upon thee, when thou doest righteousness, and his ears will be then open unto thy prayers, and he will not destroy thy memory out of the land of the living; thou shalt cry, and he will hear thee, and out of thy tribulations deliver thee; for Christ cloth never despise a heart that is contrite and humbled with fear of him. Otherwise, the worm of thy torture shall not die, and the fire of thy burning shall never be extinguished.

32

And thou too, Cuneglasse, why art thou fallen into the filth of thy former naughtiness, yea, since the very first spring of thy tender youth, thou bear, thou rider and ruler of many, and guider of the chariot which is the receptacle of the bear, thou contemner of God, and vilifier of his order, thou tawny butcher, as in the Latin tongue thy name signifies. Why dost thou raise so great a war as well against men as also against God himself, against men, yea, thy own countrymen, with thy deadly weapons, and against God with thine infinite offences? Why, besides thine other innumerable backslidings, having thrown out of doors thy wife, dost thou, in the lust, or rather stupidity of thy mind, against the apostle's express prohibition, denouncing that no adulterers can be partakers of the kingdom of heaven, esteem her detestable sister, who had vowed unto God the everlasting contineney, as the very dower (in the language of the poet) of the celestial nymphs? Why cost thou provoke with thy frequent injuries the lamentations and sighs of saints, by thy means corporally afflicted, which will in time to come, like a fierce lioness, break thy bones in pieces? Desist, I beseech thee (as the prophet saith) from wrath, and leave off thy deadly fury, which thou breathest out against heaven and earth, against God and his flock, and which in time will be thy own torment; rather with altered mind obtain the prayers of those who possess a power of binding over this world, when in this world they bind the guilty, and of loosing when they loose the penitent. Be not (as the apostle saith) proudly wise, nor hope thou in the uncertainty of riches, but in God who giveth thee many things abundantly, and by the amendment of thy manners purchase unto thyself a good foundation for hereafter, and seek to enter into that real and true state of existence which will be not transitory but everlasting. Otherwise, thou shalt know and see, yea, in this very world, how bad and bitter a thing it is for thee to leave the Lord thy God, and not have his fear before shine eyes, and in the next, how thou shalt be burned in the foul encompassing flames of endless fire, nor yet by any manner of means shalt ever die. For the souls of the sinful are as eternal in perpetual fire, as the souls of the just in perpetual joy and gladness.

33

And likewise, O thou dragon of the island, who hast deprived many tyrants, as well of their kingdoms as of their lives, and though the last-mentioned in my writing, the first in mischief, exceeding many in power, and also in malice, more liberal than others in giving, more licentious in sinning, strong in arms, but stronger in working thine own soul's destruction, Maglocune, why art thou (as if soaked in the wine of the Sodomitical grape) foolishly rolling in that black pool of shine offences? Why dost thou wilfully heap like a mountain, upon thy kingly shoulders, such a load of sins? Why dost thou show thyself unto the King of kings who hath made thee as well in kingdom as in stature of body higher than almost all the other chiefs of Britain) not better likewise in virtues than the rest; but on the contrary for thy sins much worse? Listen then awhile and hear patiently the following enumeration of thy deeds, wherein I will not touch any domestic and light offences (if yet any of them are light) but only those open ones which are spread far and wide in the knowledge of all men. Didst not thou, in the very beginning of thy youth, terribly oppress with sword, spear, and fire, the king thine uncle, together with his courageous bands of soldiers, whose countenances in battle were not unlike those of young lions? Not regarding the words of the prophet, who says, "The blood-thirsty and deceitful men shall not live out half their days," and even if the sequel of thy sins were not such as ensued, yet what retribution couldst thou expect for this offence only at the hands of the just Judge, who hath said by his prophet: "Woe be to thee who spoilest, and shalt not thou thyself be spoiled? and thou who killest, shalt not thyself be killed? and when thou shalt make an end of thy spoiling, then shalt thou thyself fall."

34

But when the imagination of thy violent rule had succeeded according to thy wishes, and thou west urged by a desire to return into the right way, night and day the consciousness of thy crimes afflicted thee, whilst thou didst ruminate on the Lord's ritual and the ordinances of the monks, and then publish to the world and vow thyself before God a monk with no intention to be unfaithful, as thou didst say, having burst through those toils in which such great beasts as thyself were used to become entangled, whether it were love of rule, of gold, or silver, or, what is stronger still, the fancies of thy own heart. And didst thou not, as a dove which cleaves the yielding air with its pinions, and by its rapid turns escapes the furious hawk, safely return to the cells where the saints repose, as a most certain place of refuge? Oh how great a joy should it have been to our mother church, if the enemy of all mankind had not lamentably pulled thee, as it were, out of her bosom! Oh what an abundant flame of heavenly hope would have been kindled in the hearts of desperate sinners, hadst thou remained in thy blessed estate! Oh what great rewards in the kingdom of Christ would have been laid up for thy soul against the day of judgment, if that crafty wolf had not caught thee, who of a wolf wast now become a lamb (not much against thine own will) out of the fold of our Lord, and made thee of a lamb, a wolf like unto himself, again? Oh how great a joy would the preservation of thy salvation have been to God the Father of all saints had not the devil, the father of all castaways, as an eagle of monstrous wings and claws, carried I thee captive away against all right and reason, to the unhappy band of his children? And to be short, thy conversion to righteousness gave as great joy to heaven and earth, as now thy detestable return, like a dog to his vomit, breedeth grief and lamentation: which being done, "the members which should have been busily employed, as the armour of justice for the Lord, are now become the armour of iniquity for sin and the devil;" for now thou dost not listen to the praises of God sweetly sounded forth by the pleasant voices of Christ's soldiers, nor the instruments of ecclesiastical melody, but thy own praises (which are nothing) rung out after the fashion of the giddy rout of Bacchus by the mouths of thy villainous followers, accompanied with lies and malice, to the utter destruction of the neighbours, so that the vessel prepared for the service of God, is now turned to a vessel of dirt, and what was once reputed worthy of heavenly honour, is now cast as it deserves into the bottomless pit of hell.

35

Yet neither is thy sensual mind (which is overcome by the excess of thy follies) at all checked in its course with committing so many sins, but hot and prone (like a young colt that coveteth every pleasant pasture) runneth headlong forward, with irrecoverable fury, through the intended fields of crime, continually increasing the number of its transgressions. For the former marriage of thy first wife (although after thy violated vow of religion she was not lawfully thine, but only by right of the time she was with thee), was now despised by thee, and another woman, the wife of a man then living, and he no stranger, but thy own brother's son, enjoyed thy affections. Upon which occasion that stiff neck of thine (already laden with sins) is now burdened with two monstrous murders, the one of thy aforesaid nephew, the other, of her who once was thy wedded wife: and thou art now from low to lower, and from bad to worse, bowed, bent, and sunk down into the lowest depth of sacrilege. Afterwards, also didst thou publicly marry the widow by whose deceit and suggestion such a heavy weight of offences was undergone, and take her, lawfully, as the flattering tongues of thy parasites with false words pronounced it, but as we say, most wickedly, to be thine own in wedlock. And therefore what holy man is there, who, moved with the narration of such a history, would not presently break out into weeping and lamentations? What priest (whose heart lieth open unto God) would not instantly, upon hearing this, exclaim with anguish in the language of the prophet: "Who shall give water to my head, and to my eyes a fountain of tears, and I will day and night bewail those of my people, who are slaughtered." For full little (alas!) hast thou with thine ears listened to that reprehension of the prophet speaking in this wise: "Woe be unto you, O wicked men, who have left the law of the most holy God, and if ye shall be born, your portion shall be to malediction, and if ye die, to malediction shall be your portion, all things that are from the earth, to the earth shall be converted again, so shall the wicked from malediction pass to perdition:" if they return not unto our Lord, listening to this admonition: "Son, thou hast offended; add no further offence thereunto, but rather pray for the forgiveness of the former." And again, "Be not slow to be converted unto our Lord, neither put off the same from day to day, for his wrath doth come suddenly." Because, as the Scripture saith, "When the king heareth the unjust word, all under his dominion become wicked." And, the just king (according to the prophet) raiseth up his region.

36

But warnings truly are not wanting to thee, since thou hast had for thy instructor the most eloquent master of almost all Britain. Take heed, thereof, lest that which Solomon noteth, befall thee, which is, "Even as he who stirreth up a sleeping man out of his heavy sleep, so is that person who declareth wisdom unto a fool, for in the end of his speech will he say, What hast thou first spoken? Wash thine heart (as it is written) from malice, O Jerusalem, that thou mayest be saved." Despise not (I beseech thee) the unspeakable mercy of God, calling by his prophet the wicked in this way from their offences: "I will on a sudden speak to the nation, and to the kingdom, that I may root out, and disperse, and destroy, and overthrow." As for the sinner he doth in this wise exhort him vehemently to repent. "And if the same people shall repent from their offence, I will also repent of the evil which I have said that I would do unto them." And again, "Who will give them such an heart, that they may hear me, and keep my commandments, and that it may be well with them all the days of their lives." And also in the Canticle of Deuteronomy, "A people without counsel and prudence, I wish they would be wise, and understand, and foresee the last of all, how one pursueth a thousand and two put to flight ten thousand." And again, our Lord in the gospel, "Come unto me, all ye who do labour and are burdened, and I will make you rest. Take my yoke upon you, and learn of me, because I am meek and humble of heart, and ye shall find repose for your souls." For if thou turn a deaf ear to these admonitions, contemn the prophets, and despise Christ, and make no account of us, humble though we be, so long as with sincere piety and purity of mind we bear in mind that saying of the prophet, that we may not be found, "Dumb dogs, not able to bark;" (however I for my part may not be of that singular fortitude in the spirit and virtue of our Lord, as to declare, "To the house of Jacob their sins, and the house of Israel their offences;") and so long as we shall remember that of Solomon, "He who says that the wicked are just, shall be accursed among the people, and odious to nations, for they who reprove them shall have better hopes." And again, "Respect, not with reverence thy neighbour in his ruin, nor forbear to speak in time of salvation." And as long also as we forget not this, "Root out those who are led to death, and forbear not to redeem them who are murdered;" because, as the same prophet says, "Riches shall not profit in the day of wrath, but justice delivereth from death." And, "If the just indeed be hardly saved, where shall the wicked and sinner appear? If as I said, thou scorn us, who obey these texts, the dark flood of hell shall without doubt eternally drown thee in that deadly whirlpool, and those terrible streams of fire that shall ever torment and never consume thee, and then shall the confession of thy pains and sorrow for thy sins be altogether too late and unprofitable to one, who now in this accepted time and day of salvation deferreth his conversion to a more righteous way of life.

37

And here, indeed, if not before, was this lamentable history of the miseries of our time to have been brought to a conclusion, that I might no further discourse of the deeds of men; but that I may not be thought timid or weary, whereby I might the less carefully avoid that saying of Isaiah, "Woe be to them who call good evil, and evil good placing darkness for light, and light for darkness, bitter for sweet, and sweet for bitter, who seeing see not, and hearing hear not, whose hearts are overshadowed with a thick and black cloud of vices; "I will briefly set down the threatenings which are denounced against these five aforesaid lascivious horses, the frantic followers of Pharaoh, through whom his army is wilfully urged forward to their utter destruction in the Red Sea, and also against such others, by the sacred oracles, with whose holy testimonies the frame of this our little work is, as it were, roofed in, that it may not be subject to the showers of the envious, which otherwise would be poured thereon. Let, therefore, God's holy prophets, who are to mortal men the mouth of God, and the organ of the Holy Ghost, forbidding evils, and favouring goodness, answer for us as well now as formerly, against the stubborn and proud princes of this our age, that they may not say we menace them with such threats, and such great terrors of our own invention only, and with rash and over-zealous meddling. For to no wise man is it doubtful how far more grievous the sins of this our time are than those of the primitive age, when the apostle said, "Any one transgressing the law, being convicted by two or three witnesses, shall die, how much worse punishment think ye then that he deserveth, who shall trample under his foot the Son of God?"

38

And first of all appears before us, Samuel, by God's commandment, the establisher of a lawful kingdom, dedicated to God before his birth, undoubtedly known by marvellous signs, to be a true prophet unto all the people, from Dan even to Beersheba, out of whose mouth the Holy Ghost thundereth to all the potentates of the world, denouncing Saul the first king of the Hebrews, only because he did not accomplish some matters commanded him of our Lord, in these words which follow: "Thou hast done foolishly neither yet hast thou kept the commandments of our Lord thy God, that he hath given thee in charge; which if thou hadst not committed, even now had our Lord prepared thy reign over Israel for ever, but thy kingdom shall no farther arise." And what did he commit, whether it were adultery or murder, like to the offences of the present time? No, truly, but broke in part one of God's commandments, for, as one of our writers says, "The question is not of the quality of the sin, but of the violating of the precept." Also when he endeavoured to answer (as he thought): the objections of Samuel, and after the fashion of men wisely to make excuses for his offence in this manner: "Yea, I have obeyed the voice of our Lord, and walked in the way I through which he hath sent me;" with this rebuke was he corrected by him: "What! will our Lord have burnt offerings or oblations, and not rather that the voice of our Lord should be obeyed? Obedience is better than oblations, and to hearken unto him, better than to offer the fat of rams. For as it is the sin of soothsaying to resist, so is it the offence of idolatry not to obey; in regard, therefore, that thou hast cast away the word of our Lord, he hath also cast thee away that thou be not king." And a little after, "Our Lord hath this day rent the kingdom of Israel from thee, and delivered it up to thy neighbour, a man better than thyself. The Triumpher of Israel truly will not spare, and will not be bowed with repentance, neither yet is he a man that he should repent;" that is to say, upon the stony hearts of the wicked: wherein it is to be noted how he saith, that to be disobedient unto God is the sin of idolatry. Let not, therefore, our wicked transgressors (while they do not openly sacrifice to the gods of the Gentiles) flatter themselves that they are not idolaters, whilst they tread like swine the most precious pearls of Christ under their feet.

39

But although this one example as an invincible affirmation might abundantly suffice to correct the wicked; yet, that by the mouths of many witnesses all the offences of Britain may be proved, let us pass to the rest. What happened to David for numbering his people, when the prophet had spake unto him in this sort? Thus saith our Lord: "The choice of three things is offered thee, choose which thou wilt, that I may execute it upon thee. Shall there befall thee a famine for seven years, or shalt thou flee three months before thine enemies, and they pursue thee, or shall there be three days' pestilence in thy land?" For being brought into great straits by this condition, and willing rather to fall into the hands of God who is merciful, than into those of men, he was humbled with the slaughter of seventy thousand of his subjects, and unless with the affection of an apostolic charity, he had desired to die himself for his countrymen, that the plague might not further consume them, saying, "I am he that has offended, I the shepherd have dealt unjustly: but these sheep, what have they sinned? Let thy hand, I beseech thee, be turned against me, and against the house of my father;" he would have atoned for the unadvised pride of his heart with his own death. For what does the scripture afterwards declare of his son? "And Solomon wrought that which was not pleasing before our Lord, and he did not fill up the measure of his good deeds by following the Lord like his father David. And our Lord said unto him, Because thou hast thus behaved thyself, and not observed my covenant and precepts, which I have commanded thee, breaking it asunder; I will divide thy kingdom, and give the same unto thy servant."

40

Hear now likewise what fell upon the two sacrilegious kings of Israel (even such as ours are), Jeroboam and Baasha, unto whom the sentence and doom of our Lord is by the prophet in this way directed: "For what cause have I exalted thee a prince over Israel, in regard that they have provoked me by their vanities. Behold I will stir up after Baasha and after his house, and I will give over his house as the house of Jeroboam the son of Nebat. Who so of his blood shall die in the city, the dogs shall eat him, and the dead carcass of him that dieth in the field shall the fowls of the air eat." What cloth he also threaten unto that wicked king of Israel, a worthy companion of the former, by whose collusion and his wife's deceit, innocent Naboth was for his father's vineyard put to death, when the holy mouth of Elias, yea, the selfsame mouth that was instructed with the fiery speech of our Lord, thus spake unto him: "Hast thou killed and also taken possession, and after this wilt thou yet add more? Thus saith our Lord, in this very place, wherein the dogs have licked the blood of Naboth, they shall lick up thy blood also." Which fell out afterwards in that very sort, as we have certain proof. But lest perchance (as befell Ahab also) the lying spirit, which pronounceth vain things in the mouths of your prophets may seduce you, hearken to the words of the prophet Micaiah: "Behold God hath suffered the spirit of lying to possess the mouths of all thy prophets that do here remain, and our Lord hath pronounced evil against thee." For even now it is certain that there are some teachers inspired with a contrary spirit, preaching and affirming rather what is pleasing, however depraved, than what is true: whose words are softer than oil, and the same are darts, who say, peace, peace, and there shall be no peace to them, who persevere in their sins, as says the prophet in another place also, "It is not for the wicked to rejoice, saith our Lord."

41

Azarias, also, the son of Obed, spoke unto Asa, who returned from the slaughter of the army of ten hundred thousand Ethiopians, saying, "Our Lord is with you while you remain with him, and if you will seek him out, he will be found by you, and if you will leave him, he will leave you also." For if Jehosaphat for only assisting a wicked king, was thus reproved by the prophet Jehu, the son of Ananias, saying, "If thou givest aid to a sinner, or lovest them whom our Lord doth hate, the wrath of God doth therefore hang over thee," what shall become of them who are fettered in the snares of their own offences? whose sin we must of necessity hate, if not their souls, if we wish to fight in the army of the Lord, according to the words of the Psalmist, "Hate ye evil, who love our Lord." What was said to Jehoram, the son of the above-named Jehosaphat, that most horrible murderer (who being himself a bastard, slew his noble brethren, that he might possess the throne in their place, by the prophet Elias, who was the chariot and charioteer of Israel? "Thus speaketh the Lord God of thy father David. Because thou hast not walked in the way of thy father Jehosaphat, and in the ways of Asa the king of Judah, but hast walked in the ways of the kings of Israel, and in adultery according to the behaviour of the house of Ahab, and hast moreover killed thy brethren, the sons of Jehosaphat, men far better than thyself, behold, our Lord shall strike thee and thy children with a mighty plague." And a little afterwards, "And thou shalt be very sick of a disease of thy belly, until thy entrails shall, together with the malady itself, from day to day, tome forth out of thee." And listen also what the prophet Zachariah, the son of Jehoiades, menaced to Joash, the king of Israel, when he abandoned our Lord even as ye now do, and the prophet spoke in this manner to the people: "Thus saith our Lord, Why do ye transgress the commandments of our Lord and do not prosper? Because ye have left our Lord, he will also leave you."

42

What shall I mention of Isaiah, the first and chief of the prophets, who beginneth his prophecy, or rather vision, in this way: "Hear, O ye heavens, and O thou earth conceive in shine ears, because our Lord hath spoken, I have nourished children, and exalted them, but they themselves have despised me. The ox hath known his owner, and the ass his master's crib, but Israel hath not known me, and my people hath not understood." And a little further with threatenings answerable to so great a folly, he saith, "The daughter of Sion shall be utterly left as a tabernacle in the vineyard, and as a hovel in the cucumber garden, and a city that is sacked." And especially, convening and accusing the princes, he saith, "Hear the word of our Lord, O ye princes of Sodom, perceive ye the law of our Lord, O ye people of Gomorrah." Wherein it is to be noted, that unjust kings are termed the princes of Sodom, for our Lord, forbidding sacrifices and gifts to be offered to him by such persons, and seeing that we greedily receive those offerings which in all nations are displeasing unto God, and to our own destruction suffer them not to be bestowed on the poor and needy, speak thus to them who, laden with riches, are likewise given to offend on this head: "Offer no more your sacrifice in vain, your incense is abomination unto me." And again he denounceth them thus: "And when ye shall stretch out your hands, I will turn away mine eyes from you, and when ye shall multiply your prayers, I will not hear." And he declareth wherefore he does this, saying, "Your hands are full of blood." And likewise showing how he may be appeased, he says, "Be ye washed, be ye clean, take away the evil of your thoughts from mine eyes: cease to do evil, learn to do well: seek for judgment, succour the oppressed, do justice to the pupil or orphan." And then assuming as it were the part of a reconciling mediator, he adds, "Though your sins shall be as scarlet, they shall be made white as snow: though they shall be as red as the little worm, they shall be as white as wool. If ye shall be willing to hear me, ye shall feed on the good things of the land; but if ye will not, but provoke me unto wrath, the sword shall devour you."

43

Receive ye the true and public avoucher, witnessing, without any falsehood or flattery, the reward of your good and evil, not like the soothing humble lips of your parasites, which whisper poisons into your ears. And also directing, his sentence against ravenous judges, he saith thus: "Thy princes are unfaithful, companions of thieves, all love gifts, hunt after rewards: they do no justice to the orphan, the widow's cause entereth not unto them. For thus saith our Lord God of hosts, the strong one of Israel, Alas, I will take consolation upon my foes, and be revenged upon mine enemies; and the heinous sinners shall be broken to powder, and offenders together with them, and all who have left our Lord, shall be consumed." And afterwards, "The eyes of the lofty man shall be brought low, and the height of men hath bowed down." And again, "Woe be to the wicked, evil befall him, for he shall be rewarded according to his handy-work." And a little after, "Woe be unto you who arise early to follow drunkenness, and to drink even to the very evening, that ye may fume with wine. The harp, and the lyre, and the tabor, and the pipe, and wine are in your banquets, and the work of our Lord ye respect not, neither yet consider ye the works of his hands. Therefore is my people led captive away, because they have not had knowledge, and their nobles have perished with famine, and their multitude hath withered away with thirst. Therefore hath hell enlarged and dilated his spirit, and without measure opened his mouth, and his strong ones, and his people, and his lofty and glorious ones, shall descend down unto him." And afterwards, "Woe be unto you who are mighty for the drinking of wine, and strong men for the procuring of drunkenness, who justify the wicked for rewards, and deprive the just man of his justice. For this cause even as the tongue of the fire devoureth the stubble, and as the heat of the flame burneth up, so shall their root be as the ashes, and their branch shall rise up as the dust. For they have cast away the law of our Lord of hosts, and despised the speech of the holy one of Israel. In all these the fury of our Lord is not turned away, but as yet his hand is stretched out."

44

And further on, speaking of the day of judgment and the unspeakable fears of sinners, he says, "Howl ye, because the day of our Lord is near at hand (if so near at that time, what shall it now be thought to be?) for destruction shall proceed from God. For this shall all hands be dissolved, and every man's heart shall wither away, and be bruised; tortures and dolours shall hold them, as a woman in labour so shall they be grieved, every man shall at his neighbour stand astonished, burned faces shall be their countenances. Behold, the day of our Lord shall come, fierce and full of indignation, and of wrath, and fury, to turn the earth into a desert, and break her sinners in small pieces from off her; because the stars of heaven and the brightness of them, shall not unfold their light, the sun in his rising shall be covered over with darkness, and the moon shall not shine in her season; and I will visit upon the evils of the world, and against the wicked, their own iniquity, and I will make the pride of the unfaithful to cease, and the arrogancy of the strong, I will bring low." And again, "Behold our Lord will disperse the earth, and he will strip her naked, and afflict her face, and scatter her inhabitants; and as the people, so shall be the priest; and as the slave, so shall be his lord; as the handmaid, so shall be her lady; as the purchaser, so shall be the seller; as the usurer, so shall be he that borroweth; as he who demandeth, so shall he be that oweth. With dispersing shall the earth be scattered, and with sacking shall she be spoiled. For our Lord hath spoken this word. The earth hath bewailed, and hath flitted away; the world hath run to nothing, she is weakened by her inhabitants, because they have transgressed laws, changed right, brought to ruin tile eternal truce. For this shall malediction devour the earth."

45

And afterwards, "They shall lament all of them who now in heart rejoice, the delight of the timbrels hath ceased, the sound of the gladsome shall be silent, the sweetness of the harp shall be hushed, they shall not with singing drink their wine, bitter shall be the potion to the drinkers thereof. The city of vanity is wasted, every house is shut up, no man entering in; an outcry shall be in the streets over the wine, all gladness is forsaken, the joy of the land is transferred, solitariness is left in the town, and calamity shall oppress the gates, because these things shall be in the midst of the land, and in the midst of the people." And a little further, "Swerving from the truth, they have wandered out of the right way, with the straggling of transgressors have they gone astray. Fear and intrapping falls, and a snare upon thee who art the inhabitant of the earth. And it shall come to pass: whoso shall flee from the voice of the fear, shall tumble down into the intrapping pit; and whoso shall deliver himself out of the downfall, shall be caught in the entangling snare: because the food-gates from aloft shall be opened, and the foundations of the earth shall be shaken. With bruising shall the earth be broken, with commotion shall she be moved, with tossing shall she be shaken like a drunken man, and she shall be taken away as if she were a pavilion of one night's pitching, and her iniquities shall hang heavy upon her, and she shall fall down, and shall not attempt to rise again. And it shall be, that our Lord in the same day shall look on the warfare of heaven on high, and on the kings of the earth, who are upon the earth, and they shall be gathered together in the bundle of one burden into the lake, and shall there be shut up in prison, and after many days shall they be visited. And the moon shall blush, and the sun be confounded, when our Lord of hosts shall reign in Mount Sion and in Jerusalem, and be glorified in the sight of his seniors."

46

And after a while, giving a reason why he threateneth in that sort, he says thus: "Behold the hand of our Lord is not shortened that he cannot save, neither is his ear made heavy that he may not hear. But your iniquities have divided between you and your God, and your offences have hid his face from you, that he might not hear. For your hands are defiled with blood, and your fingers with iniquity: your lips have spoken lying, and your tongue uttereth iniquity. There is none who calleth on justice, neither is there he who judgeth truly, but they trust in nothing, and speak vanities, and have conceived grief, and brought forth iniquity." And a little after, "Their works are unprofitable, and the work of iniquity is in their hands; their feet run into evil, and make haste that they may shed the innocent blood; their thoughts are unprofitable thoughts, spoil and confusion are in their ways, and the way of peace they have not known, and in their steps there is no judgment, their paths are made crooked unto them, every one who treadeth in them is ignorant of peace; in this respect is judgment removed far off from you, and justice taketh no hold on you." And after a few words, "And judgment hath been turned back, and justice hath stood afar oft, because truth hath fallen down in the streets, and equity could not enter in; and truth is turned into oblivion, and whoso hath departed from evil, hath lain open to spoil. And our Lord hath seen, and it was not pleasing in his eyes, because there is not judgment."

47

And thus far may it suffice among many, to have recited a few sentences out of the prophet Isaiah.

But now with diligent ears hearken unto him, who was foreknown before he was formed in the belly, sanctified before he came out of the womb, and appointed a prophet in all nations: I mean Jeremiah, and hear what he hath pronounced of foolish people and cruel kings, beginning his prophecy in his mild and gentle manner.

"And the word of God was spoken unto me, saying, Go and cry in the ears of Jerusalem, and thou shalt pronounce, Hear the word of our Lord, thou house of Jacob, and all ye kindred of the house of Israel: Thus saith our Lord; What iniquity have your fathers found in me, who have been far removed from me, and walked after vanity, and are become vain, and have not said, Where is he who made us go up out of the land of Egypt?" And after a few words, "From the beginning of thine age thou hast broken my yoke, violated my bands, and said, I will not serve, I have planted thee my chosen vine, all true seed. How art thou therefore converted into naughtiness? O strange vine! If thou shalt wash thee with nitre, and multiply unto thee the herb borith, thou art spotted in my sight with thine iniquity, saith our Lord." And afterwards, "Why will ye contend with me in judgment? Ye have all forsaken me, saith our Lord in vain have I corrected your children, they have not received discipline. Hear ye the word of our Lord. Am I made a solitariness unto Israel, or a late bearing land! why therefore hath my people said, we have departed, we will come no more unto thee? Doth the virgin forget her ornament, or I the spouse her gorget? my people truly hath forgotten me for innumerable days. Because my people are foolish, they I have not known me, they are unwise and mad children. They are wise to do evil, but to do well they have been ignorant."

48

Then the prophet speaketh in his own person saying, "O Lord thine eyes do respect faith, thou hast stricken them, and they have not sorrowed, thou hast broken them and they have refused to receive discipline, they have made their faces harder than the rock, and will not return." And also our Lord: "Declare ye this same to the house of Jacob, and make it to be heard in Judah, saying, Hear, ye foolish people who have no heart, who having eyes see not, and ears hear not. Will ye not therefore dread me, saith our Lord, and will ye not conceive grief from my countenance, who have placed the sand as the bound of the sea, an eternal commandment which she shall not break, and her waves, shall be moved, and they cannot, and her surge shall swell and yet not pass the same? But to this people is framed an incredulous and an exasperating heart, they have retired and gone their ways, and not in their heart said, Let us fear our Lord God." And again, "Because there are found among my people wicked ones, framing wiles to entangle as if they were fowlers, setting snares and gins to catch men: as a net that is full of birds, so are their houses filled with deceits. Therefore are they magnified and enriched, they are become gross and fat, and have neglected my speeches most vilely, the orphans' cause they have not decided, and the justice of the poor they have not adjudged. What! shall I not visit these men, saith our Lord? or shall not my soul be revenged upon such a nation?"

49

But God forbid that ever should happen unto you, that which followeth, "Thou shalt speak all these words unto them, and they shall not hear thee; and thou shalt call them, and they shall not answer thee; and thou shalt say unto them, This is the nation that hath not heard the voice of their Lord God, nor yet received discipline, faith hath perished, and been taken away from out of their mouth." And after some few speeches, "Whoso falleth doth he not arise again, and whoso is turned away, shall he not return again? why therefore is this people in Jerusalem, with a contentious aversion alienated? they have apprehended lying, and they will not come back again. I have been attentive, and hearkened diligently, no man speaketh what is good. There is none who repenteth of his sin, saying, What have I done? All are turned unto their own course, like a horse passing with violence to battle. The kite in the sky hath known her time, the turtle, and swallow, and stork have kept the season of their coming, but my people hath not known the judgment of God." And the prophet, being smitten with fear at so wonderful a blindness, and unspeakable drunkenness of the sacrilegious, and lamenting them who did not lament themselves (even according to the present behaviour of these our unfortunate tyrants), beseecheth of our Lord, that an augmentation of tears might be granted him, speaking in this manner, "I am contrite upon the contrition of the daughter of my people, astonishment hath possessed me is there no balm in Gilead, or is: there no physician there? Why therefore is not the wound of the daughter of my people healed? Who shall give water unto my head, and to mine eyes a fountain of tears, arid I will day and night bewail the slaughtered of my people? who will grant me in the wilderness the inn of passengers? and I will utterly leave my people, and depart from them; because they are all of them adulterers, a root of offenders, and they have bent their tongue as the bow of lying, and not of truth, they are comforted in the earth, because they have passed from evil to evil, and not known me, saith our Lord." And again: "And our Lord hath said, Because they have forsaken my law, which I have given them, and not heard my voice, nor walked thereafter, and have wandered away after the wickedness of their own heart, in that respect our Lord of hosts, the God of Israel, saith these words, Behold I will feed this people with wormwood, and give them to drink the water of gall." And a little after (speaking in the person of God), "See therefore thou do not pray for this people, nor assume thou for them praise and prayer, because I will not hear in the time of their outcry unto me, and of their affliction."

50

What then shall now our miserable governors do, these few who found out the narrow way and left the large, were by God forbidden to pour out their prayers for such as persevered in their evils, and so highly provoked his wrath, against whom on the contrary side when they returned with all their hearts unto God (his divine Majesty being unwilling that the soul of man should perish, but calling back the castaway that he should not utterly be destroyed) the same prophets could not procure the heavenly revenge, because Jonas, when he desired the like most earnestly against the Ninevites, could not obtain it. But in the meanwhile omitting our own words, let us rather hear what the prophetic trumpet soundeth in our ears speaking thus: "If thou shalt say in thy heart, Why have these evils befallen? For the multitude of thine iniquities. If the Ethiopian can change his skin, or the leopard his sundry spots, ye may also do well when ye have learned evil," ever supposing that ye will not. And afterwards: "These words doth our Lord say to this people, who have loved to move their feet, and have not rested, and not pleased our Lord, Now shall he remember their iniquities, and visit their offences; and our Lord said unto me, Pray thou not for this people to work their good, when they fast, I will not hear their prayers; and if they offer burnt sacrifices and oblations, I will not receive them." And again, "And our Lord said unto me, If Moses and Samuel shall stand before me, my soul is not bent to this people, cast them out away from my face, and let them depart." And after a few words: "Who shall have pity on thee Jerusalem, or who shall be sorrowful for thee, or who shall pray for thy peace? Thou hast left me (saith our Lord) and gone away backward, and I will stretch forth my hand over thee, and kill thee." And somewhat after: "Thus saith our Lord, Behold I imagine a thought against you, let every man return from his evil course, and make straight your ways and endeavours, who said, we despair, we will go after our own thoughts, and every one of us will do the naughtiness of his evil heart. Thus therefore saith our Lord, Ask the Gentiles, who hath heard such horrible matters, which the virgin Israel hath too often committed? Shall there fail from the rock of the field, the snow of Libanus? or can the waters be drawn dry that gush out cold and flowing? because my people hath forgotten me." And somewhat also after this propounding unto them an election, he speaking saith, "Thus saith our Lord, Do ye judgment and justice, and deliver him who by power is oppressed out of the hand of the malicious accuser; and for the stranger, and orphan, and widow, do not provoke their sorrow, neither yet work ye unjustly the grief of others, nor shed ye forth the innocent blood. For if indeed ye shall accomplish this word, there shall enter in through the gates of this house, kings of the lineage of David, sitting upon his throne. But if ye will not hearken unto these words, by myself I have sworn (saith our lord) that this house shall be turned into a desert." And again (for he spoke of a wicked king), "As I live (saith our Lord) if so be that Jechonias shall be a ring on my right hand, I will pluck him away, and give him over into the hands of them who seek his life."

51

Moreover, holy Abraham crieth out, saying, "Woe be unto them who build a city in blood, and prepare a town in iniquities, saying, Are not these things from our almighty Lord? and many people have failed in fire, and many nations nave been diminished." And thus complaining, he begins his prophecy: "How long, O Lord, shall I call, and thou wilt not hear? Shall I cry out unto thee, to what end hast thou given me labours and griefs, to behold misery and impiety?" And on the other side, "And judgment was sat upon, and the judge hath taken in regard hereof, the law is rent in pieces, and judgment is not brought fully to his conclusion, because the wicked through power treadeth the just under foot. In this respect hath passed forth perverse judgment."

52

And mark ye also what blessed Hosea the prophet says of princes: "For that they have transgressed my covenant, and ordained against my law, and exclaimed, we have known thee, because thou art against Israel. They have persecuted good, as if it were evil. They have reigned for themselves and not by me; they have held a principality, neither yet have they acknowledged me."

53

And hear ye likewise the holy prophet Amos, in this sort threatening: "In three heinous offences of the sons of Judah, and in four I will not convert them, for that they have cast away the law of our Lord, and not kept his commandments, but their vanities have seduced them. And I will send fire upon Judah, and it shall eat the foundations of Jerusalem. Thus saith our Lord, In three grievous sins of Israel, and in four I will not convert them, for that they have sold the just for money, and the poor man for shoes, which they tread upon the dust of the earth, and with buffets they did beat the heads of the poor, and have eschewed the way of the humble." And after a few words, "Seek our Lord and ye shall live, that the house of Joseph may not shine as fire, and the flame devour it, and he shall not be, that can extinguish it. The house of Israel hath hated him who rebuketh in the gates, and abhorred the upright word." Which Amos, being forbidden to prophesy in Israel, without any fawning flattery, saith in answer, "I was not a prophet, nor yet the son of a prophet, but a goatherd; I was plucking sycamores and our Lord took me from my herd, and our Lord said unto me, Go thy way and prophesy against my people of Israel: and now hear thou the word of our Lord (for he directed his speech unto the king), thou sayest, do not prophesy against Israel, and thou shalt not assemble troops against the house of Jacob. For which cause our Lord saith thus, thy wife in the city shall play the harlot, and thy sons and daughters shall die by the sword, and thy ground be measured by the cord, and thou in a polluted land shalt end thy life, but for Israel, she shall be led from his own country a captive." And afterwards, "Hear therefore these words, ye who do outrageously afflict the poor, and, practise your mighty power against the needy of the earth, who say, when shall the month pass over that we may purchase, and the sabbaths that we may open the treasuries." And within a few words after, "Our Lord doth swear against the pride of Jacob, if he shall in contempt forget your actions, and if in these the earth shall not be disturbed, and end every inhabitant thereof fall to lamentation, and the final end as a flood ascend, and I will turn your festival days into wailing, and cast haircloth on the loins of every one, and on the head of every man baldness, and make him as the mourning of one over beloved, and those who are with him as the day of his sorrow." And again, "In the sword shall die all the sinners of my people, who say, evils shall not approach nor yet shall light upon us."

54

And listen ye, likewise, what holy Michah the prophet hath spoken, saying, "Hearken, ye tribes. And what shall adorn the city? Shall not fire? and the house of the wicked hoarding up unjust treasures, and with injury unrighteousness? If the wrongful dealer shall be justified in the balance, and deceitful weights in the scales by which they have heaped up their riches in ungodliness."

55

And hear also what threats the famous prophet Zephaniah thundereth out: saith he, "The great day of our Lord is near; it is at hand, and very swiftly approacheth. The voice of the day of our Lord is appointed to be bitter and mighty, that day, a day of wrath, a day of tribulation and necessity, a day of clouds and mist, a day of the trumpet and outcry, a day of misery and extermination, a day of darkness and dirtiness upon the strong cities and high corners. And I will bring men to tribulation, and they shall go as if they were blind, because they have offended our Lord, and I will pour out their blood as dust, and their flesh as the dung of oxen, and their silver and gold shall not be able to deliver them in the day of the wrath of our Lord. And in the fire of his zeal shall the whole earth be consumed, when the Lord shall accomplish his absolute end, and bring solitariness upon all the inhabitants of the earth. Come together and be joined in one, thou nation without discipline, before ye be made as the fading flower, before the wrath of our Lord falleth upon ye."

56

And give ear also unto that which the prophet Haggai speaketh: "Thus saith our Lord, I will once move the heaven, and earth, and sea, and dry land, and I will drive away the thrones of kings, and root out the power of the kings of the Gentiles, and I will chase away the chariots of those who mount upon them."

57

Now also behold what Zacharias the son of Addo, that chosen prophet, said, beginning his prophecy in this manner: "Return to me, and I will return unto you, saith our Lord, and be not like your fathers, to whom the former prophets have imputed, saying, Thus saith our almighty Lord, Turn away from your ways, and they have not marked whereby they might obediently hear me." And afterwards, "And the angel asked me, what dost thou see? And I said, I see a flying scythe, which containeth in length twenty cubits. The malediction which hath proceeded upon the face of the whole earth; because every one of her thieves shall be punished even to the death, and I will throw him away, saith our almighty Lord, and he shall enter into the house of fury, and into the house of swearing falsehood in my name."

58

Holy Malachy the prophet also saith, "Behold, the day of our Lord shall come, inflamed as a furnace, and all proud men, and al workers of iniquity shall be as stubble, and the approaching day of the Lord of hosts shall set them on fire, which shall not leave a root nor a bud of them."

59

And hearken ye also what holy Job debateth of the beginning and end of the ungodly, saying, "For what purpose do the wicked live, and have grown old dishonestly, and their issue hath been according to their own desire, and their sons before their faces, and their houses are fruitful, and no fear nor yet the scourge of our Lord is upon them. Their cow hath not been abortive, their great with young hath brought forth her young ones and not missed, but remaineth as an eternal breed; and their children rejoice, and taking the psaltery and harp, have finished their days in felicity and fallen peaceably asleep down into hell." Doth God, therefore, not behold the works of the wicked? Not so, truly, "But the candle of the ungodly shall be extinguished, and destruction shall fall upon them, and pains as of one in childbirth, shall withhold them from wrath; and they shall be as chaff before the wind, and as the dust which the whirlwind hath carried away. Let all goodness fail his children; let his eyes behold his own slaughter, nor yet by our Lord let him be redeemed." And a little after, he saith of the same men, "Who have ravenously taken the flock with the shepherd, and driven away the beast of the orphans, and engaged the ox of the widow, and deceiving, have declined from the way of necessity. They have reaped other men's fields before the time; the poor have laboured in the vineyards of the mighty without hire and meat, they have made many to sleep naked without garments; of the covering of their life they have bereaved them." And somewhat afterwards, when he had thoroughly understood their works, he delivered them over to darkness. "Let, therefore, his portion be accursed from the earth; let his plantings bring forth witherings; let him for this be rewarded according to his dealings; let every wicked man like the unsound wood be broken in pieces. For arising in his wrath hath he overthrown the impotent. Wherefore truly shall he have no trust of his life; when he shall begin to grow diseased, let him not hope for health, but fall into languishing. For his pride hath been the hurt of many, and he is become decayed and rotten, as the mallows in the scorching heat, or as the ear of corn when it falleth off from its stubble." And afterwards, "If his children shall be many, they shall be turned to the slaughter, and if he gather together silver as if it were earth, and likewise purify his gold as if it were dirt, all these same shall the just obtain."

60

Hear ye moreover what blessed Esdras, that cyclopaedia of the divine law, threateneth in his discourse. "Thus saith our Lord God: My right hand shall not be sparing upon sinners, neither shall the sword cease over them who spill the innocent blood on the earth. Fire shall proceed from out of my wrath, and devour the foundations of the earth, and sinners as if they were inflamed straw. Woe be unto them who offend, and observe not my commandments, saith our Lord, I will not forbear them. Depart from me ye apostatizing children, and do not pollute my sanctuary. God doth know who offend against him, and he will therefore deliver them over to death and to slaughter. For now have many evils passed over the round compass of the earth. A sword of fire is sent out against you, and who is he that shall restrain it? shall any man repulse a lion that hungereth in the wood? or shall any one quench out the fire when the straw is burning? our Lord God will send out evils, and who is he that shall repress them? and fire will pass forth from out of his wrath, and who shall extinguish it? it shall brandishing shine, and who will not fear it? it shall thunder, and who will not shake with dread? God will threaten all, and who will not be terrified? before his face the earth doth tremble, and the foundations of the sea shake from the depths."

61

And mark ye also what Ezechiel the renowned prophet, and admirable beholder of the four evangelical creatures, speaketh of wicked offenders, unto whom pitifully lamenting beforehand the scourge that hung over Israel, our Lord doth say, "Too far hath the iniquity of the house of Israel and Judah prevailed, because the earth is filled with iniquity and uncleanness. Behold I am, mine eyes shall not spare, nor will I take pity." And afterwards, "Because the earth is replenished with people, and the city fraughted with iniquity, I will also turn away the force of their power, and their holy things shall be polluted, prayer shall approach and sue for peace, and it shall not be obtained." And somewhat after, "The word of our Lord, quoth he, was spoken unto me, saying, Thou son of man, the land that shall so far sin against me as to commit an offence, I will stretch forth my hand upon her, and break in pieces her foundation of bread, and send upon her famine, and take away mankind and cattle from her; and if these three men, Noah, Daniel, and Job, be in the midst of her, they shall not deliver her, but they in their justice shall be saved, saith our Lord. If so be that also I shall bring in evil beasts upon the land and punish her, she likewise shall be turned to destruction, and there shall not be one who shall have free passage from the face of the beasts, and although these three men are in the midst of her, as I live, saith our Lord, their sons and daughters shall not be I preserved, but they alone shall be saved, and as for the land it shall fall to confusion." And again, "The son shall not receive the unrighteousness of the father, neither the father the son's unrighteousness. The justice of the just shall be upon himself. And the unjust man, if he turneth him away from all the iniquities which he hath done, and keepeth all my commandments, and doth justice and abundance of mercy he shall live in life and shall not die. All his sins, whatsoever he hath committed, shall have no further being; he shall live the life in his own justice which he hath performed. Do I with my will voluntarily wish the death of the unrighteous, saith our Lord, rather than that he should return from his evil way and live? But when the just shall turn himself away from his justice, and do iniquity, according to all the iniquities which the unrighteous hath committed, all the just actions (which he hath done) shall remain no further in memory. In his offence wherein he hath fallen, and in his sins in which he hath transgressed, he shall die." And, within some words afterwards: " And all nations shall understand, that the house of Israel are led captive away for their offences, because they have forsaken me. And I have turned my face from them, and yielded them over into the hands of their enemies, and all have perished by the sword; according unto their unclean sins, and after their iniquities have I dealt with them, and turned my face away from them."

62

This which I have spoken may suffice concerning the threats of the holy prophets: only I have thought it necessary to intermingle in this little work of mine, not only these menaces, but also a few words borrowed out of the wisdom of Solomon, to declare unto kings matters of exhortation or instruction, that they may not say I am willing to load the shoulders of men with heavy and insupportable burdens of words, but not so much as once with mine own finger (that is, with speech of consolation) to move the same. Let us therefore hear what the prophet hath spoken to rule us. "Love justice," saith he, "ye that judge the earth." This testimony alone (if it were with a full and perfect heart observed) would abundantly suffice to reform the governors of our country. For if they had loved justice, they would also love God, who is in a sort the fountain and original of all justice. "Serve our Lord in goodness, and seek him in simplicity of heart." Alas! who shall live (as a certain one before us hath said) when such things are done by our countrymen, if perchance they may be any where accomplished? "Because he is found of those who do not tempt him, he appeareth truly to them who have faith in him." For these men without respect do tempt God, whose commandments with stubborn despite they contemn, neither yet do they keep to him their faith, unto whose oracles be they pleasing, or somewhat severe, they turn their backs and not their faces. "For perverse thoughts do separate from God," and this in the tyrants of our time very plainly appeareth. But why doth our meanness intermeddle in this so manifest a determination? Let therefore him who alone is true (as we have said) speak for us, I mean the Holy Ghost, of whom it is now pronounced, "The Holy Ghost verily will avoid the counterfeiting of discipline." And again, "Because the Spirit of God hath filled the globe of the earth." And afterwards (showing with an evident judgment the end of the evil and righteous) he saith, "How is the hope of the wicked as the down that is blown away with the wind, and as the smoke that with the blast is dispersed, and as the slender froth that with a storm is scattered, and as the memory of a guest who is a passenger of one day. But the just shall live forever, and with God remaineth their reward, and their cogitation is with the Highest. Therefore shall they receive the kingdom of glory, and the crown of beauty from the hand of our Lord. Because with his right hand he will protect them, and with his holy arm defend them." For very far unlike in quality are the just and ungodly, as our Lord verily hath spoken, saying, "Them who honour me I will honour, and whoso despise me shall be of no estimation."

63

But let us pass over to the rest: "Hearken, (saith he) all ye kings, and understand ye; learn, ye judges of the bounds of the earth, listen with your ears who keep multitudes in awe, and please yourselves in the troops of nations. Because power is given unto you from God, and puissance from the highest, who will examine your actions, and sift your thoughts. For that when ye were ministers of his kingdom, ye have not judged uprightly, nor kept the law of justice, nor yet walked according to his will. It shall dreadfully and suddenly appear unto you, that a most severe judgment shall be given on them who govern. For to the meaner is mercy granted, but the mighty shall mightily sustain torments. For he shall have no respect of persons, who is the ruler of all, nor yet shall he reverence the greatness of any one, because he himself hath made both small and great, and care alike he hath of all; but for the stronger is at hand a stronger affliction. Unto you therefore, O kings, are these my speeches, that you may learn wisdom, and not fall away from her. For whoso observeth what things are just shall be justified, and whoso learneth what things are holy, shall be sanctified."

64

Hitherto have we discoursed no less by the oracles of the prophets, than by her own speeches with the kings of our country, being willing they should know what the prophet hath spoken, saying, "As from the face of a serpent, so fly thou from sins: if thou shalt approach unto them they will catch thee, their teeth are the teeth of a lion, such as kill the souls of men." And again, "How mighty is the mercy of our Lord, and his forgiveness to such as turn unto him." And if we have not in us such apostolical zeal, that we may say, "I did verily desire to be anathematized by Christ for my brethren," notwithstanding that we may from the bottom of our hearts speak that prophetic saying, "Alas! that the soul perisheth." And again, "Let us search out our ways, and seek and return unto our Lord: let us lift our hearts together with our hands to God in heaven." And also that of the apostle, "We covet that every one of you should be in the bowels of Christ."

65

And how willingly, as one tossed on the waves of the sea, and now arrived in a desired haven, would I in this place make an end (shame forbidding me further to proceed), did I not behold such great masses of evil deeds done against God by bishops or other priests, or clerks, yea some of our own order, whom as witnesses myself must of necessity first of all stone (according unto the law) with the hard blows of words, lest I should be otherwise reproved for partiality towards persons, and then afterwards the people (if as yet they keep their decrees) must pursue with their whole powers the same execution upon them, not to their corporal death, but to the death of their vices and their eternal life with God. Yet, as I before said, I crave pardon of them, whose lives I not only praise, but also prefer before all earthly treasure, and of the which, if it may be, yet before my death I desire and thirst to be a partaker: and so having both my sides defended with the double shields of saints, and by those means invincibly strengthened to sustain all that arise against me, arming moreover my head in place of a helmet with the help of our Lord, and being most assuredly protected with the sundry aids of the prophets, I will boldly proceed notwithstanding the stones of worldly rioters fly never so fast about me.

66

Britain hath priests, but they are unwise; very many that minister, but many of them impudent; clerks she hath, but certain of them are deceitful raveners; pastors (as they are called) but rather wolves prepared for the slaughter of souls (for they provide not for the good of the common people, but covet rather the gluttony of their own bellies), possessing the houses of the church, but obtaining them for filthy lucre's sake; instructing the laity, but showing withal most depraved examples, vices, and evil manners; seldom sacrificing, and seldom with clean hearts, standing at the altars, not correcting the commonality for their offences, while they commit the same sins themselves; despising the commandments of Christ, and being careful with their whole hearts to fulfil their own lustful desires, some of them usurping with unclean feet the seat of the apostle Peter; but for the demerit of their covetousness falling down into the pestilent chair of the traitor Judas; detracting often, and seldom speaking truly; hating verity as an open enemy, and favouring falsehoods, as their most beloved brethren; looking on the just, the poor, and the impotent, with stern countenances, as if they were detested serpents, and reverencing the sinful rich men without any respect of shame, as if they were heavenly angels, preaching with their outward lips that alms are to be disbursed upon the needy, but of themselves not bestowing one halfpenny; concealing the horrible sins of the people, and amplifying injuries offered unto themselves, as if they were done against our Saviour Christ; expelling out of their houses their religious mother, perhaps, or sisters, and familiarly and indecently entertaining strange women, as if it were for some more secret office, or rather, to speak truly, though fondly (and yet not fondly to me, but to such as commit these matters), debasing themselves unto such bad creatures; and after all these seeking rather ambitiously for ecclesiastical dignities, than for the kingdom of heaven; and defending after a tyrannical fashion their achieved preferments, nor even labouring with lawful manners, to adorn the same; negligent and dull to listen to the precepts of the holy saints (if ever they did so much as once hear that which full often they ought to hear), but diligent and attentive to the plays and foolish fables of secular men, as if they were the very ways to life, which indeed are but the passages to death; being hoarse, after the fashion of bulls, with the abundance of fatness, and miserably prompt to all unlawful actions; bearing their countenances arrogantly aloft, and having nevertheless their inward senses, with tormenting and gnawing consciences; depressed down to the bottom or rather to the bottomless pit; glad at the gaining of one penny, and at the loss of the like value sad; slothful and dumb in the apostolical decrees (be it for ignorance or rather the burden of their offences), and stopping also the mouths of the learned, but singularly experienced in the deceitful shifts of worldly affairs; and many of this sort and wicked conversation, violently intruding themselves into the preferments of the church; yea, rather buying the same at a thigh rate, than being any way drawn thereunto, and moreover as unworthy wretches, wallowing, after the fashion of swine, in their old and unhappy puddle of intolerable wickedness, after they have attained unto the seat of the priesthood or episcopal dignity (who neither have been installed, or resident on the same), for usurping only the name of priesthood, they have not received the orders or apostolical preeminence; but how can they who are not as yet fully instructed in faith, nor have done penance for their sins, be any way supposed meet and convenient to ascend unto any ecclesiastical degree (that I may not speak of the highest) which none but holy and perfect men, and followers of the apostles, and, to use the words of the teacher of the Gentiles, persons free from reprehension, can lawfully and without the foul offence of sacrilege undertake.

67

For what is so wicked and so sinful as after the example of Simon Magus (even if with other faults he had not been defiled before), for any man with earthly price to purchase the office of a bishop or priest, which with holiness and righteous life alone ought lawfully to be obtained; but herein they do more wilfully and desperately err, in that they buy their deceitful and unprofitable ecclesiastical degrees, not of the apostles or their successors, but of tyrannical princes, and their father the devil; yea, rather they raise this as a certain roof and covering of all offences, over the frame of their former serious life, that being protected under the shadow thereof, no man should lightly hereafter lay to their charge their old or new wickedness; and hereupon they build their desires of covetousness and gluttony, for that being now the rulers of many they may more freely make havoc at their pleasure. For if truly any such offer of purchasing ecclesiastical promotions were made by these impudent sinners (I will not say with St. Peter), but to any holy priest, or godly king, they would no doubt receive the same answer which their father Simon Magus had from the mouth of the apostle Peter, saying: "Thy money be with thee unto thy perdition." But, alas! perhaps they who order and advance these ambitious aspirers, yea, they who rather throw them under foot, and for a blessing give them a cursing, whilst of sinners they make them not penitents (which were more consonant to reason), but sacrilegious and desperate offenders, and in a sort install Judas, that traitor to his Master, in the chair of Peter, and Nicholas, the author of that foul heresy, in the seat of St. Stephen the martyr, it may be at first obtained their own priesthood by the same means, and therefore do not greatly dislike in their children but rather respect the course, that they their fathers did before follow. And also, if finding resistance, in obtaining their dioceses at home, and some who severely renounce this chaffering of church-livings, they cannot there attain to such a precious pearl, then it doth not so much loath as delight them (after they have carefully sent their messengers beforehand) to cross the seas, and travel over most large countries, that so, in the end, yea even with the sale of their whole substance, they may win and compass such a pomp, and such an incomparable glory, or to speak more truly, such a dirty and base deceit and illusion. And afterwards with great show and magnificent ostentation, or rather madness, returning back to their own native soil, they grow from stoutness to stateliness, and from being used to level their looks to the tops of the mountains, they now lift up their drowsy eyes into the air, even to the highest clouds, and as Novatus, that foul hog, and persecutor of our Lord's precious jewel, did once at Rome, so do these intrude themselves again into their own country, as creatures of a new mould, or rather as instruments of the devil, being even ready in this state and fashion to stretch out violently their hands (not so worthy of the holy altars as of the avenging flames of hell) upon Christ's most holy sacrifices.

68

What do you therefore, O unhappy people! expect from such belly beasts? (as the apostle calleth them). Shall your manners be amended by these, who not only do not apply their minds to any goodness, but according to the upbraiding of the prophet, labour also to deal wickedly? Shall ye be illuminated with such eyes as are only with greediness cast on those things that lead headlong to vices (that is to say), to the gates of hell? Nay truly, if according to the saying of our Saviour, ye flee not these most ravenous wolves like those of Arabia, or avoid them as Lot, who ran most speedily from the fiery shower of Sodom up to the mountains, then, being blind and led by the blind, ye will both together tumble down into the infernal ditch.

69

But some man perchance will objecting say, that all bishops or all priests (according to our former exception), are not so wickedly given, because they are not defiled with the infamy of schism, pride, or unclean life, which neither we ourselves will deny, but albeit we know them to be chaste, and virtuous, yet will we briefly answer.

What did it profit the high-priest Hely, that he alone did not violate the commandments of our Lord, in taking flesh with forks out of the pots, before the fat was offered unto God, while he was punished with the same revenge of death wherewith his sons were? What one, I beseech you, of them, whose manners we have before sufficiently declared, hath been martyred like Abel, from malicious jealousy of his more acceptable sacrifice, which with the heavenly fire ascended up into the skies, since they fear the reproach even of an ordinary word? Which of them "hath hated the counsel of the malicious, and not sat with the ungodly," so that of him as a prophet, the same might be verified which was said of Enoch, "Enoch walked with God and was not to be found" in the vanity (forsooth) of the whole world, as then leaving our Lord, and beginning to halt after idolatry? Which of them, like Noah in the time of the deluge, hath not admitted into the ark of salvation (which is the present church) any adversary unto God, that it may be most apparent that none but innocents or singular penitents, ought to remain in the house of our Lord? Who is he that offering sacrifice like Melchisedeck, hath only blessed the conquerors, and them who with the number of three hundred (which was in the sacrament of the Trinity) delivering the just man, have overthrown the deadly armies of the five kings, together with their vanquishing troops, and not coveted the goods of others? Which of them hath like Abraham, at the commandment of God freely offered his own son on the altar to be slain, that he might accomplish a precept of Christ, agreeable to this saying, Thy right eye, if it cause thee to offend, ought to be pulled out; and another of the prophet, That he is accursed who withholdeth his sword from shedding blood? Who is he that like Joseph, hath rooted out of his heart the remembrance of an offered injury? Who is he that like Moses, speaking with our Lord in the mountain, and not there terrified with the sounding trumpets, hath in a figurative sense presented unto the incredulous people the two tables, and his horned face which they could not endure to see, but trembled to behold ? Which of them, praying for the offences of the people, has from the very bottom of his heart cried out, like unto him, saying: "O Lord this people hath committed a grievous sin, which if thou wilt forgive them, forgive it; otherwise blot me guilty out of thy book?"

70

Which of them, inflamed with the admirable zeal of God, hath courageously risen to punish fornication, curing without delay by the present medicine of penance, the affection of filthy lust, lest the fire of the wrath of God should otherwise consume the people, as Phineas the priest did, that by these means justice for ever might be reputed unto him? Which of them hath in moral understanding imitated Joshua, the son of Nun, either for the utter rooting forth, even to the slaughter of the last and least of all, the seven nations out of the land of promise, or for the establishing of spiritual Israel in their places? Which of them hath showed unto the people of God their final bounds beyond Jordan that it might be known what was suited to every tribe, in such sort as the aforenamed Phineas and Jesus have wisely divided the land? Who is he that to overthrow the innumerable thousands of Gentiles, adversaries to the chosen people of God, hath, as another Jephtha, for a votive and propitiatory sacrifice, slain his own daughter (by which is to be understood his own proper will), imitating also therein the apostle, saying, "Not seeking what is profitable to me, but to many, that they may be saved;" which daughter of his met the conquerors with drums and dances, by which are to be understood the lustful desires of the flesh? Which of them, that he might disorder, put to flight, and overthrow the camps of the proud Gentiles, by the number of three hundred, (being, as we before said, the mystery of the blessed Trinity,) and with his men holding in their hands those noble sounding trumpets, (which are prophetical and apostolical senses, according as our Lord said to the prophet, "Exalt thy voice as a trumpet;" and the psalmist of the apostles, "Their sound hath passed throughout the whole earth,") and bearing all those famous flagons shining in the night with that most glittering fiery light, (which are to be interpreted the bodies of saints joined to good works, and burning with the flame of the Holy Ghost, yea having, as the apostle writes, "This treasure in earthen vessels,") hath after hewing down the idolatrous grave (by which is morally meant dark and foul desire) marched on like Gideon, with an assured faith in the evident sign of the fleece, which to the Jews was void of the heavenly moisture, but to the Gentiles made wet with the dew of the Holy Ghost?

71

Who is he among them that (earnestly wishing to die to this world, and live to Christ) hash, as another Sampson, utterly cut off such innumerable luxurious banqueters of the Gentile, while they praised their gods, (by which is meant, while the senses of men extolled these earthly riches, according to the apostle speaking thus: "And covetousness, which is idolatry"), shaking with the power of both his arms the two pillars (by which are to be understood the wicked pleasures of the soul and body), by which the house of all worldly wickedness is in a sort compacted and underpropped? Which of them, like Samuel, with prayers and the burnt sacrifice of a sucking lamb, hath driven away the fear of the Philistines, raised unexpected thunderclaps, and showering clouds, established without flattery a king, deposed him when he displeased God, and anointed another his better in his place and kingdom; and when he shall give to the people his last farewell, shall appear like Samuel in this sort, saying, "Behold, I am ready, speak ye before our Lord and his anointed, whether I ever took away the ox or ass of any man, if I have falsely accused any one, if I have oppressed anybody, if I have received a bribe from the hands of any?" Unto whom it was answered by the people, "Thou hast not wrongfully charged us, nor oppressed us, nor taken anything from the hands of any." Which of them, like the famous prophet Elias, who consumed with heavenly fire the hundred proud men, and preserved the fifty that humbled themselves; and afterwards denounced without flattery or dissimulation, the impending death of the unjust king (that sought not the counsel of God by his prophets, but of the idol Accaron), hath utterly overthrown all the prophets of Baal (by which are meant the worldly senses ever bent, as we have already said, to envy and avarice), with the lightning sword (which is the word of God)? And as the same Elias, moved with the zeal of God, after taking away the showers of rain from the land of the wicked, who were now shut up with famine in a strong prison, as it were of penury, for three years and six months, being himself ready to die for thirst in the desert, hath, complaining, said, "They have murdered, O Lord, thy prophets, and undermined thine altars, and I alone am left, and they seek my life?"

72

Which of them, like Elisha, hath punished his dearly beloved disciple, if not with an everlasting leprosy, yet at least by abandoning him, if burdened too much with the weight of worldly covetousness for those very gifts which his master before (although very earnestly entreated thereto) had despised to receive? And which of these among us hath like him revealed unto his servant, (who despaired of life, and on a sudden trembled at the warlike army of the enemies that besieged the city wherein he was), through the fervency of his prayers poured out unto God, those spiritual visions, so that he might behold a mountain replenished with a heavenly assisting army, of warlike chariots and horsemen, shining with fiery countenances, and that he might also believe that he was stronger to save, than the foe to hurt? And which of them, like the above-named Elisha, with the touch of his body, being dead to the world, but living unto God, shall raise up another, whose fate had been different from his, namely, death to God, but life to his vices, so that instantly revived, he may yield humble thanks to Christ for his unexpected recovery from the hellish torments of his mortal crimes? Which of them hath his lips purified and made clean with the fiery coals carried by the tongues of the cherubim, from off the altar, (that his sins may be wiped away with the humility of confession), as it is written of Esaias, by whose effectual prayers, together with the aid of the godly king Ezechias, a hundred fourscore and five thousand of the Assyrian army, through the stroke of one angel, without the least print of any appearing wound, were overthrown and slain? Which of them, like blessed Jeremiah, for accomplishing the commandments of God,- for denouncing the threats thundered out from heaven, and for preaching the truth even to such as would not hear the same, hath suffered loathsome stinking prisons as momentary deaths? And to he brief, what one of them (as the teacher of the Gentiles said) hath endured like the holy prophets to wander in mountains, in dens, and caves of the earth, to be stoned, to be sawn in sunder, and assailed with all kinds of death, for the name of our Lord?

73

But why do we dwell in examples of the Old Testament as if there were none in the New? Let, therefore, those, who suppose they can, without any labour at all, under the naked presence of the name of priesthood, enter this strait and narrow passage of Christian religion, hearken unto me while I recite and gather into one a few of the chiefest flowers out of the large and pleasant meadow of the saintly soldiers of the New Testament. Which of you (who rather sleep than lawfully sit in the chair of the priesthood), being cast out of the council of the wicked, hath, after the stripes of sundry rods, like the holy apostles, from the bottom of his heart, given thanks to the blessed Trinity that he was found worthy to suffer disgrace for Christ's true deity? What one, for the undoubted testimony of God, having his brains dashed out with the fuller's club, hath, like James the first, a bishop of the New Testament, suffered corporal death? Which of you, like James the brother of John, has by the unjust prince been beheaded? Who, like the first deacon and martyr of the gospel, (having but this only accusation, that he saw God, whom the wicked could not behold), has ungodly hands been stoned to death? What one of you, like the worthy keeper of the keys of the heavenly kingdom, has been nailed to the cross with his feet upward, in reverence for Christ, whom, no less in his death than in his life, he endeavoured to honour, and hath so breathed his last? Which of you, for the confession of the true word of Christ, hath, like the vessel of election, and chosen teacher of the Gentiles, after suffering imprisonment and shipwreck, after the terrible scourges of whips, the continual dangers of seas of thieves, of Gentiles, of Jews, and of false apostles, after the labours of famine, fasting, and watching, after incessant care over all the churches, after his trouble for such as scandalized, after his infirmity for the weak, after his wonderful travels over almost the whole world in preaching the gospel of Christ, lost his head at last by the stroke of the descending sword ?"

74

Which of you, like the holy martyr Ignatius, bishop of the city of Antioch, hath after his miraculous actions in Christ, for testimony of him been torn by the jaws of lions, as he was once at Rome? whose words, as he was led to his, passion, when you shall hear (if ever your countenances were overcome with blushing), you will not only, in comparison of him, esteem yourselves no priests, but not so much even as the meanest Christians; for in the epistle which he sent to the church of Rome, he writeth thus: "From Syria even unto Rome, I fight with beasts, by land and sea, being bound and chained unto ten leopards, I mean the soldiers appointed for my sustody, who for our benefit bestowed upon them become more cruel, but I am the better instructed by their wickedness, neither yet am I in this justified; oh! when shall those beasts come the workers of my salvation, which are for me prepared? when shall they be let loose at me? when shall it be lawful for my carcass to enjoy them? whom I do most earnestly wish to be eagerly enraged against me, and truly I will incite them to devour me; moreover, I will humbly pray, lest perchance they should dread to touch my body (as in some others they have before done), yea also, if they hesitate, I will offer violence, I will force myself upon them. Pardon me, I beseech you, I know what is commodious for me, even now I begin to be the disciple of Christ; let all envy, whether of human affection or spiritual wickedness cease, that I may endeavour to obtain Christ Jesus; let fires, let crosses, let cruelty of beasts, let breaking of bones, and rending of limbs, with all the pains of the whole body, and all the torments devised by the art of the devil, be together poured out on me alone, so that I may merit to attain unto Christ Jesus." Why do you behold these things with the sleepy eyes of your souls? why do you hearken unto them with the deaf ears of your senses? Shake off, I beseech you, the dark and black mist of slothfulness from your hearts, that so you may see the glorious light of truth and humility. A Christian, and he not mean, but a perfect one, and a priest not base, but one of the highest, a martyr of no ordinary sort, but one of the chiefest, saith: "Now I begin to be the disciple of Christ." And you, like the same Lucifer, who was thrown down out of heaven, are puffed up with words, and not with power, and after a sort do chew under the tooth, and make presence in your actions, as the author of this your wickedness hath thus expressed: "I will mount up into the heavens, and be like unto the Highest." And again: "I have digged and drunk water, and dried up with the steps of my feet all the rivers of the banks." You would more rightly have imitated him and hearkened unto his words, who is without doubt the most true example of all goodness and humility, saying by his prophet, "I am verily a worm and not a man, the reproach of men, and the outcast of the people." Oh unspeakable matter! that he called himself "the reproach of men," when he washed away the reproaches of the whole world. And again in the gospel; "I am not able to do any thing of myself," when at the same time he was co-eternal with the Father, coequal with the Holy Ghost, and consubstantial with both, and created, not by the help of another, but by his own almighty power, the heaven and earth, with all their inestimable ornaments; and ye nevertheless have arrogantly lifted up your voices, notwithstanding the prophet saith, "Why do earth and ashes swell with pride?"

75

But let us return unto our subject. Which of you, I say, like Polycarp, the famous bishop of the church of Smyrna, that witness of Christ, hath courteously entertained as guests at his table, those who violently drew him out to be burned? and when for the charity which he did bear unto Christ, he was brought to the stake, said, "He who gave me grace to endure the torment of the fire, will likewise grant me without fastening of nails to bear the flames with patience." And now passing over in this my discourse the mighty armies of saints, I will yet touch on one only, for example's sake, Basil the bishop of Caesaria, who when he was thus by the unrighteous prince threatened that, unless he would on the next day be as the rest, defiled in the dirty dunghill of the Arian heresy, he should be put to death, answered, as it is reported, "I will be to-morrow the same as to-day, and for thee, I do not wish thee to change thy determination." And again, "Would that I had some worthy reward to bestow on him that would discharge Basil from the bands of this breathing bellows." Which one of you doth endeavour to daunt the menaces of tyrants, by inviolably keeping the rule of the apostolical speech, which in all times and ages hath been observed by all holy priests, to suppress the suggestion of men when they sought to draw them into wickedness, saying in this manner; "It behoveth us to obey God rather than men."

76

Wherefore after our accustomed manner, taking refuge in the mercy of our Lord, and in the sentences of his holy prophets, that they on our behalf may now level the darts of their oracles at imperfect pastors (as before at tyrants), so that thereby they may receive compunction and be amended, let us see what manner of threats our Lord doth by his prophets utter against slothful and dishonest priests, and such as do not, both by examples and words, rightly instruct the people. For even Eli, the priest in Shilo, because he did not severely proceed, with a zeal worthy of God, in punishing his sons, when they contemned our Lord, but, as a man overswayed with a fatherly affection? too mildly and remissly admonished them, was sentenced with this judgment by the prophet speaking unto him: "Thus saith our Lord; I have manifestly showed myself unto the house of thy father, when they were the servants of Pharaoh in Egypt, and have chosen the house of thy father out of all the tribes of Israel, for a priesthood unto me." And a little after, "Why hast thou looked upon mine incense, and upon my sacrifice, with a dishonest eye? and hast honoured thy children more than me, that thou mightest bless them from the beginning in all sacrifices in my presence? And now so saith our Lord: Because whoever honoureth me I will honour him again; and whoso maketh no account of me shall be brought to nothing. Behold the days shall come, and I will destroy thy name, and the seed of thy father's house. And let this be to thee the sign, which shall fall upon thy two sons, Hophni and Phineas, in one day shall they both die by the sword of men." If thus therefore they shall suffer, who correct them that are under their charge, with words only and not with condign punishment, what shall become of those who by offending exhort you, and draw others unto wickedness?

77

It is apparent also what befell unto the true prophet, who was sent from Judah to prophesy in Bethel, and forbidden to taste any meat in that place, after the sign which he foretold was fulfilled, and after he had restored to the wicked king his withered hand again, being deceived by another prophet, as he was termed, and so make to take but a little bread and water, his host speaking in this sort unto him: *Thus saith our Lord God: Because thou hast been disobedient to the mouth of our Lord, and hast not observed the precept which the Lord thy God hath commanded, and hast returned, and eaten bread, and drunk water in this place, in which I have charged thee that thou shouldest neither eat bread nor drink water, thy body shall not be buried in the sepulchre of thy forefathers. And so (saith the scripture) it came to pass, that after he had eaten bread and drunk water, he made ready his ass, and departed, and a lion found him in the way and slew him."*

78

Hear ye also the holy prophet Isaias, how he speaketh of priests on this wise. "Woe be to the ungodly, may evil befall him; for the reward of his hands shall light upon him. Her own exactors have spoiled my people, and women have borne sway over her. O my people, they who term thee blessed, themselves deceive thee, and destroy the way of thy footsteps. Our Lord standeth to judge, and standeth to judge the people. Our Lord will come unto judgment with the elders of the people and her princes. Ye have consumed my vine, the spoil of the poor is in your house. Why do ye break in pieces my people, and grind the faces of the poor? saith our Lord of hosts." And also; "Woe be unto them who compose ungodly laws, and in their writing have written injustice, that they may oppress the poor in judgment, and work violence to the cause of the lowly of my people, that widows may be their prey, and they make spoil of the orphans; what will ye do in the day of visitation and calamity approaching from afar off?" And afterwards: "But these also in regard of wine have been ignorant, and in respect of drunkenness have wandered astray; the priests have not understood, because of drunkenness, and have been swallowed up in wine, they have erred in drunkenness, they have not known him who seeth, they have been ignorant of judgment. For all tables are filled with the vomit of their uncleanness, in so much as there is not any free place to be found."

79

"Hear therefore the word of our Lord, O ye deceivers, who bear authority over my people that is in Jerusalem. For ye have said, We have entered into a truce with death, and with hell we have made a covenant. The overflowing scourge when it shall pass forth shall not fall upon us, because we have placed falsehood for our hope, and by lying we have been defended." And somewhat after: "And hail shall overthrow the hope of lying, together with the defence. Waters shall overflow, and your truce with death shall be destroyed, and your covenant with hell shall not continue, when the overflowing scourge shall pass forth; ye shall also be trodden under foot, whensoever it shall pass along through you, it shall sweep you away withal." And again: "And our Lord hath said: Because this people approacheth with their mouth, and with their lips glorify me, but their heart is far from me; behold, therefore, I will cause this people to wonder by a great and stupendous miracle. For wisdom shall decay and fall away from her wise men, and the understanding of her sages shall be concealed. Woe be unto you that are profound in heart, to conceal counsel from our Lord, whose works are in darkness, and they say, who seeth us? And who hath known us? for this thought of yours is perverse." And afterwards: "Thus saith our Lord, Heaven is my seat, and the earth my footstool. What is this house that ye will erect unto me, and what place shall be found for my resting-place? all these things hath my hand made, and these universally have been all created, saith our Lord. On whom truly shall I cast mine eye, but on the humble poor man, and the contrite in spirit, and him that dreadeth my speeches? he that sacrificeth an ox, is as he that killeth a man; he that slaughtereth a beast for sacrifice, is like him who beateth out the brains of a dog; he that offereth an oblation, is as he that offereth the blood of a hog; he that is mindful of frankincense, is as he that honoureth an idol: of all these things have they made choice in their ways, and in their abominations hath their soul been delighted."

80

Hear also what Jeremy, that virgin prophet, speaketh unto the unwise pastors in this sort: "Thus saith our Lord, What iniquity have your fathers found in me, because they have removed themselves far off from me, and walked after vanity, and are become vain?" And again: "And entering in, ye have defiled my land, and made mine inheritance abomination. The priests have not said, Where is our Lord? and the rulers of the law have not known me, and the pastors have dealt treacherously against me. Wherefore I will as yet contend in judgment with you, saith our Lord, and debate the matter with your children." And a little afterwards: "Astonishment and wonders have been wrought in the land. Prophets did preach lying, and priests did applaud with their hands, and my people have loved such matters. What therefore shall be done in her last and final ends? To whom shall I speak and make protestation that he may hear me? Behold their ears are uncircumcised, and they cannot hear. Behold the word of our Lord is uttered unto them for their reproach, and they receive it not: because I will stretch out my hand upon the inhabitants of the earth, saith our Lord. For why, from the lesser even unto the greater, all study avarice, and from the prophet even unto the priest, all work deceit, and they cured the contrition of the daughter of my people, with ignominy, saying, Peace, peace, and peace there shall not be. Confounded they are, who have wrought abomination: but they are not with confusion confounded, and have not understood how to be ashamed. Wherefore they shall fall among those who are falling, in the time of their visitation shall they rush headlong down together, saith our Lord." And again: "All these princes of the declining sort, walking fraudulently, being brass and iron, are universally corrupted, the blowing bellows have failed in the fire, the finer of metals in vain hath melted, their malicious acts are not consumed, call them refuse and reprobate silver, because our Lord hath thrown them away." And after a few words: "I am, I am, I have seen, saith our Lord. Go your ways to my place in Shilo, where my name hath inhabited from the beginning, and behold what I have done thereunto for the malice of my people Israel. And now because ye have wrought all these works, saith our Lord, and I have spoken unto you, arising in the morning, and talking, and yet ye have not heard me, and I have called you, and yet ye have not answered, I will so deal towards this house, wherein my name is now called upon, and wherein ye have confidence, and to this place which I have given unto you, and to your fathers, as I have done to Shilo, and I will cast you away from my countenance."

81

And again: "My children have departed from me, and have no abiding, and there is none who any more pitcheth my tent, and advanceth my pavilion: for the pastors have dealt fondly and not sought out our Lord. Wherefore they have not understood, and their flock hath been dispersed." And a little after: "What is the matter that my beloved hath in my houses committed many offences? shall the holy flesh take away thy maliciousness from thee, wherein thou hast glorified? our Lord shall call thy name a plentiful, fair, fruitful, goodly olive; at the sound of the speech a mighty fire hath been inflamed in her, and her orchards have been quite consumed therewith." And again: "Come ye to me, and be ye gathered together, all ye beasts of the earth, make haste to devour. Many pastors have thrown down my vine, they have trampled my part under foot, they have given over my portion which was well worthy to be desired, into a desert of solitariness." And again he speaketh: "Thus saith our Lord unto this people, which have loved to move their feet, and not rested, nor yet pleased our Lord; now shall he remember their iniquities and visit their offences. Prophets say unto them, Ye shall not see the sword, and there shall be no famine among you, but our Lord shall give true peace unto you in this place. And our Lord hath said unto me, The prophets do falsely foretell in my name; I have not sent them, nor laid my commandment on them; they prophesy unto you a dying vision, and divination together with deceitfulness, and the seducement of their own hearts. And therefore thus saith our Lord: In sword and famine shall those prophets be consumed; and the people to whom they have prophesied shall by means of the famine and sword be cast out into the streets of Jerusalem, and there shall be none to bury them."

82

And moreover: "Woe be to the pastors who destroy and rend in pieces the flock of my pasture, saith our Lord. Thus, therefore, saith our Lord God of Israel, unto the pastors who guide my people, Ye have dispersed my flock, and cast them forth, and not visited them. Behold I will visit upon you the malice of your endeavours, saith our Lord. For the prophet and the priest are both defiled, and in my house have I found their evil, saith our Lord, and therefore shall their way be as a slippery place in the dark, for they shall be thrust forward, and fall down together therein, for I will bring evils upon them, the year of their visitation, saith our Lord. And in the prophets of Samaria I have seen foolishness, and they did prophesy in Baal, and deceived my people Israel, and in the prophets of Jerusalem, have I seen the like resemblance, adultery, and the way of lying, and they have comforted the hands of the vilest offenders, that every man may not be converted from his malice: they have been all made to me as Sodom, and the inhabitants thereof as those of Gomorrha. Thus, therefore, saith our Lord to the prophets: Behold, I will give them wormwood for their food, and gall for their drink. For there hath passed from the prophet of Jerusalem pollution over the whole earth. Thus saith our Lord of hosts, Listen not to the words of prophets, who prophesy unto you, and deceive you, for they speak the vision of their own heart, and not from the mouth of our Lord. For they say unto those who blaspheme me, Our Lord hath spoken, peace shall be unto you; and to all that walk in the wickedness of their own hearts, they have said, evil shall not fall upon them. For who was present in the counsel of our Lord, and hath seen and heard his speech, who hath considered of his word, and hearkened thereunto? Behold, the whirlwind of the indignation of our Lord passeth out, and a tempest breaking forth, shall fall upon the heads of the wicked; the fury of our Lord shall not return, until the time that he worketh, and until he fulfilleth the cogitation of his heart. In the last days of all shall ye understand his counsel."

83

And little also do ye conceive and put in execution that which the holy prophet Joel hath likewise spoken in admonishment of slothful priests, and lamentation of the people's suffering for their iniquities, saying: "Awake, ye who are drunk, from your wine, and weep and bewail ye all, who have drunk wine even to drunkenness, because joy and delight are taken away from your mouths. Mourn, ye priests, who serve the altar, because the fields have been made miserable. Let the earth mourn, because corn hath become miserable, and wine been dried up, oil diminished, and husbandmen withered away. Lament ye possessions, in regard of wheat and barley, because the vintage hath perished out of the field, the vine withered up, the figs diminished; the pomegranates, and palm, and apple, and all trees of the field are withered away, in respect that the children of men have confounded their joy." All which things are spiritually to be understood by you, that your souls may not wither away with so pestilent a famine, for want of the word of God. And again, "Weep out ye priests, who serve our Lord, saying, Spare, O Lord, thy people, and give not over thine inheritance unto reproach, and let not nations hold dominion over them, that Gentiles may not say, Where is their God?" And yet ye yield not your ears unto these sayings, but admit of all matters by which the indignation of God's fury is more vehemently inflamed.

84

With diligence also attend ye what holy Hosea the prophet hath spoken unto priests of your behaviour. "Hear these words, O ye priests, and let the house of Israel, together with the king's house, mark them; fasten ye them in your ears, for unto you pertaineth judgment, because ye are made an entangling snare to the espying watch, and as a net stretched over the toils which the followers of hunting have framed."

85

To you also may this kind of alienation from our Lord be meant by the prophet Amos, saying, "I have hated and rejected your festival days, and I will not receive the savour in your solemn assemblies, because albeit ye offer your burnt sacrifices and hosts, I will not accept them, and I will not cast mine eye on the vows of your declaration. Take away from me the sound of your songs, and the psalm of your organs I will not hear." For the famine of the evangelical meat consuming, in your abundance of victuals, the very bowels of your souls, rageth violently within you, according as the aforesaid prophet hath foretold, saying, "Behold, the days shall come, saith our Lord, and I will send out a famine upon the earth; not the famine of bread, nor the thirst of water, but a famine in hearing the word of God, and the waters shall be moved from sea to sea, and they shall run over from the north even unto the east, seeking the word of our Lord, and shall not find it."

86

Let holy Micah also pierce your ears, who like a heavenly trumpet soundeth loudly forth against the deceitful princes of the people, saying, "Hearken now ye princes of the house of Jacob, Is it not for you to know judgment, who hate goodness, and seek after mischief, who pluck their skins from off men, and their flesh from their bones? Even as they have eaten the flesh of my people, and flayed their skins from them, broken their bones to pieces, and hewed them small as meat to the pot, they shall cry to God, and he will not hear them, and in that season turn his face away from them, even as they before have wickedly behaved themselves in their inventions. Thus speaketh our Lord of the prophets who seduce my people, who bite with their teeth, and preach against them peace, and if a man giveth nothing to stop their mouths, they raise and sanctify a war upon him. Night shall therefore be unto you in place of a vision, and darkness unto you in lieu of divination, and the sun shall set upon your prophets, and the day shall wax dark upon them, and seeing dreams they shall be confounded, and the diviners shall be derided, and they shall speak ill against all men, because there shall not be any one that will hear them, but that I myself shall do mine uttermost and strongest endeavour in the spirit of our Lord, in judgment and in power, that I may declare unto the house of Jacob their impieties, and to Israel their offences. Hearken, therefore, unto these words, ye captains of the house of Jacob, and ye remnants of the house of Israel, who abhor judgment, and overthrow all righteousness, who build up Sion in blood, and Jerusalem in iniquities: her rulers did judge for rewards, and her priests answered for hire, and her prophets did for money divine, and rested on our Lord, saying, And is not the Lord among us? Evils shall not fall upon us. For your cause, therefore, shall Sion be ploughed up as a field, and Jerusalem as the watch-house of a garden, and the mountain of the house as the place of a woody wilderness." And after some words ensuing: "Woe is me for that I am become as he that gathereth stubble in the harvest, and a cluster of grapes in the vintage, when the principal branch is not left to be eaten. Woe is me that a soul hath perished through earthly actions, the reverence of sinners ariseth even with reverence from the earth, and he appeareth not that shall use correction among men. All contend in judgment for blood, and every one with tribulation afflicteth his neighbour, for mischief he prepareth his hands.

87

Listen ye likewise how the famous prophet Zephaniah debated also in times past, concerning your revellers (for he spake of Jerusalem, which is spiritually to be understood the church or the soul), saying, "O the city that was beautiful and set at liberty, the confiding dove hath not hearkened to the voice, nor yet entertained discipline, she hath not trusted in our Lord, and to her God she hath not approached." And he showeth the reason why, "Her princes have been like unto roaring lions, her judges as wolves of Arabia did not leave towards the morning, her prophets carrying the spirit of a contemptuous despising man; her priests did profane what was holy, and dealt wickedly in the law, but our Lord is upright in the midst of his people, and in the morning he will not do injustice, in the morning will he give his judgment."

88

But hear ye also blessed Zachariah the prophet, in the word of God, admonishing you: "For thus saith our Almighty Lord, Judge ye righteous judgment, and work ye every one towards his brother mercy and pity, and hurt ye not through your power the widow, or orphan, or stranger, or poor man, and let not any man remember in his heart the malice of his brother; and they have been stubborn not to observe these, and have yielded their backs to foolishness, and made heavy their ears that they might not hearken, and framed their hearts not to be persuaded that they might not listen to my law and words, which our Almighty Lord hath sent in his Spirit, through the hands of his former prophets, and mighty wrath hath been raised by our Almighty Lord." And again; "Because they who have spoken, have spoken molestations, and diviners have uttered false visions and deceitful dreams, and given vain consolations; in respect hereof they are made as dry as sheep, and are afflicted because no health was to be found; my wrath is heaped upon the shepherds, and upon the lambs will I visit." And within a few words after: "The voice of lamenting pastors, because their greatness is become miserable. The voice of roaring lions, because the fall of Jordan is become miserable: thus saith our Almighty Lord: They who possessed have murdered, and yet hath it not repented them, and they who sold them, have said, Our Lord is blessed and we have been enriched, and their pastors have suffered nothing concerning them. For which I will now bear no sparing hand over the inhabitants of the earth, saith our Lord."

89

Hear ye moreover what the holy prophet Malachi denounceth unto you, saying: "Ye priests who despise my name, and have said: Wherein do we despise thy name? in offering on mine altar polluted bread: and ye have said; Wherein have we polluted it? In that ye have said: The table of our Lord is as nothing, and have despised such things as have been placed thereon; because if ye bring what is blind for an offering, is it not evil? If ye set and apply what if lame or languishing, is it not evil? Offer therefore the same unto thy governor, if he will receive it, if he will accept of thy person, saith our Almighty Lord. And now do ye humbly pray before the countenance of your God, and earnestly beseech him (for in your hands have these things been committed) if happily he will accept of your persons." And again: "And out of your ravenous theft ye have brought in the lame and languishing, and brought it in as an offering. Shall I receive the same at your hands, saith our Lord? Accursed is the deceitful man who hath in his flock one of the male kind and yet making his vow offereth the feeble unto our Lord, because I am a mighty king, saith our Lord of hosts, and my name is terrible among the Gentiles. And now unto you appertaineth this commandment, O ye priests, if ye will not hear, and resolve in your hearts to yield glory unto my name, saith our Lord of hosts, I will send upon you poverty, and accurse your blessings, because ye have not settled these things on your hearts. Behold I will stretch out my arm over ye, and disperse upon your countenances the dung of your solemnities." But that ye may in the meantime, with more zeal prepare your organs and instruments of mischief, to be converted into goodness, hearken ye (if there remain ever so little disposition to listen in your hearts) what he speaketh of a holy priest, saying "My covenant of life and peace was with him (for historically he did speak of Levi and Moses): I gave fear unto him, and he was timorous of me, he dreaded before the countenance of my name; the law of truth was in his mouth, and iniquity was not found in his lips, he walked with me in peace and equity, and turned many away from unrighteousness. For the lips of the priest shall keep knowledge, and from out of his mouth they shall require the law, because he is the Angel of our Lord of hosts." And now again he changeth his style, and ceaseth not to rebuke and reprove the unrighteous, saying: "Ye have departed from the way, and scandalized many in the law, and made void my covenant with Levi, saith our Lord of hosts. In regard whereof I have also given you over as contemptible and abject among my people, according as ye have not observed my ways, and accepted countenance of men in the law. What, is there not one Father of us all? What, hath not one God created us? Why therefore doth every one despise his brother?" And again, "Behold our Lord of hosts will come, and who can conceive the day of his coming, and who shall endure to stand to behold him? For he shall pass forth as a burning fire, and as the fuller's herb, and shall sit melting and trying silver, and ye shall purge the sons of Levi, and cleanse them as gold and as silver." And somewhat afterwards: "Your words have grown strong against me, saith our Lord, and ye have spoken thus: He is vain who serveth God, and what profit because we have kept his commandments, and walked sorrowfully before our Lord of hosts. We shall therefore now call the arrogant blessed, for because they are erected and builded up, while they work iniquity, they have tempted God, and are made safe."

90

But hear ye also what Ezechiel the prophet hath spoken, saying, "Woe upon woe shall come, and messenger upon messenger shall be, and the vision shall be sought for of the prophet, and the law shall perish from the priests, and counsel from the elders." And again: "Thus saith our Lord: In respect that your speeches are lying, and your divinations vain. For this cause, behold, I will come unto you, saith our Lord; I will stretch out my hand on your prophets, who see lies, and them who speak vain things; in the discipline of my people they shall not be, and in the Scripture of the house of Israel, they shall not be written, and into the land of Israel they shall not enter, and ye shall know that I am the Lord, because they have seduced my people, saying, The peace of our Lord, and there is not the peace of our Lord. Here have they built the wall, and they anointed it, and it shall fall." And within some words afterwards: "Woe be unto these who fashion pillows, apt for every elbow of the hand, and make veils upon every head of all ages to the subversion of souls, and the souls of my people are subverted, and they possess their souls, and contaminated me unto my people for a handful of barley, and a piece of bread to the slaughter of the souls, whom it behoved not to die, and to the delivery of the souls, that were not fit to live, while ye talk unto my people that listeneth after vain speeches." And afterwards: "Say, thou son of man, thou art earth which is not watered with rain, neither yet hath rain fallen upon thee in the day of wrath, in which thy princes were in the midst of thee as roaring lions, ravening on their prey, devouring souls in their potent might, and receiving rewards, and thy widows were multiplied in the midst of thee, and her priests have despised my law, and defiled my holy things. Between holy and polluted, they did not distinguish, and divided not equally between the unclean and clean, and from my sabbaths they veiled their eyes, and in the midst of them they defiled."

91

And again: " And I sought among them a man of upright conversation, and one who should altogether stand before my face, to prevent the times that might fall upon the earth, that I should not in the end utterly destroy it, and I found him not. And I poured out upon it, the whole design of my mind, in the fire of my wrath for the consuming of them: I repaid their ways on their heads, saith our Lord." And somewhat after: "And the word of our Lord was spoken unto me, saying: O son of man, speak to the children of my people, and they shalt say unto them: The land whereupon I shall bring my sword, and the people of the land shall take some one man among them, and ordain him to be a watchman over them, and he shall espy the sword coming upon the land, and sound with his trumpet, and signify unto the people, whoso truly shall then hear the sound of the trumpet, and yet hearing shall not beware: and the sword shall come and catch him, his blood shall light upon his own head, because when he heard the sound of the trumpet, he was not watchful, his blood shall be upon him, and this man, for that he hath preserved his own soul, hath delivered himself. But the watchman if he shall see the sword coming, and not give notice with his trumpet, and the people shall not be aware, and the sword coming shall take away a soul from among them, both tile soul itself is caught a captive for her iniquities, and I will also require her blood at the hand of the watchman. And thou, O son of man, I have appointed thee a watchman over the house of Israel, and if thou shalt hear the word from out of my mouth, when I shall say to a sinner, Thou shalt die the death, and yet wilt not speak whereby the wicked may return from his way: both the unjust himself shall die in his iniquity, and truly I will require his blood also at thy hands. But if thou shalt forewarn the wicked of his way, that he may avoid the same, and he nevertheless will not withdraw himself from his course, this man shall die in his impiety, and thou hast preserved thine own soul."

92

And so let these few among a multitude of prophetical testimonies suffice, by which the pride or sloth of our stubborn priests may be repelled, to the end they may not suppose that we act rather of our own invention, but by the authority of the laws, and saints, denounce such threats against them. And now let us also behold what the trumpet of the gospel, sounding to the whole world, speaketh likewise to disordered priests; for as we have often said, this our discourse tendeth not to treat of them, who obtain lawfully the apostolical seat, and such as rightly and skilfully understand how to dispose of their spiritual food (in time convenient) unto their fellow servants, if yet at this time there remain any great number of these in this our country; but we only talk of ignorant and unexpert shepherds, who leave their flock, and feed on vain matters, and have not the words of a learned pastor. And therefore it is an evident token that he is not a lawful pastor, yea not an ordinary Christian, who rejecteth and denieth these sayings, which are not so much ours (who of ourselves are very little worth), as the decrees of the Old and New Testament, even as one of ours right well doth say, "We do exceedingly desire that the enemies of the church should also, without any manner of truce be our adversaries: and that the friends and defenders thereof should not only be accounted our confederates, but also our fathers and governors." For let every one, with true examination, call his own conscience unto account, and so shall he easily find, whether according to true reason he possesseth his priestly chair or no. Let us see, I say, what the Saviour and Creator of the world hath spoken. "Ye are," saith he, "the salt of the earth, if that the salt vanisheth away, wherein shall it be salted? it prevaileth to no purpose any farther, but that it be cast out of doors, and trampled under the feet of men."

93

This only testimony might abundantly suffice to confute all such as are impudent; but that it may be yet, by the words of Christ, more evidently proved with what intolerable bonds of crimes these false priests entangle and oppress themselves, some other sayings are also to be adjoined; for it followeth: "Ye are the light of the world. A city placed on a mountain cannot be hid: neither do they light a candle, and put it under a bushel, but upon a candlestick, that it may shine unto all who are in the house." What priest therefore of this fashion and time, who is so possessed with the blindness of ignorance, doth, as the light of a most bright candle, shine with the lamp of learning and good works, in any house, to all that sit in the darksome night? What one is so accounted a safe public and conspicuous refuge, to all the children universally of the church, that he may be to his countrymen a defensible and strong city, situated on the top of a high mountain? Moreover, which one of them can accomplish one day together, that which followeth: "Let your light so shine before men, that they may see your good works, and glorify your Father who is in heaven:" since rather a certain most obscure cloud of theirs, and the black night of offences, hang over the island, in such a manner, that they all turn almost away from the righteous course, and make them to wander astray through unpassable and cumbersome paths of wickedness, and so their heavenly Father is not only by their works not magnified, but also by the same intolerably blasphemed. These testimonies of holy scripture, which are either already cited, or hereafter to be intermixed in this epistle, I would gladly wish to interpret in some historical or moral sense, as far as my meanness would allow.

94

But for fear lest this our little work should be immeasurably tedious unto those who despise, loathe, and disdain, not so much our speeches as God's sayings, I have already alleged, and mean hereafter to affirm these sentences plainly without any circumstance. And to proceed, within a few words after: "For whoever shall break one of the least of these commandments, and so instruct men, shall be called the least in the kingdom of heaven." And again: "Judge ye not that ye may not be judged; for in what judgment ye shall judge, ye shall be judged." And which one, I pray you, of your company will regard this same that followeth: "But why cost thou see," saith he, "the mote in thy brother's eye, and considerest not the beam in thine own eye? or how dost thou say to thy brother, suffer me to cast the mote out of thine eye, and behold the beam remaineth still in thine own eye?" Or this which follows: "Do not give what is holy to dogs, neither yet shall ye cast your pearls before swine, lest perchance they tread them under their feet, and turn again and rend you," which hath often befallen you. And, admonishing the people, that they should not by deceitful doctors, such as ye, be seduced, he saith: "Keep yourselves carefully from false prophets, who come unto you in sheep's clothing, but inwardly are ravenous wolves: by their fruit shall ye know them. Do men gather grapes of thorns, or figs of thistles? So every good tree beareth good fruit, and the evil, evil fruit." And somewhat afterward: "Not every one who saith unto me, Lord, Lord, shall enter into the kingdom of heaven; but whoso doeth the will of my Father that is in heaven, he shall enter into the kingdom of heaven."

95

And what shall then become of you, who, as the prophet hath said, believe God only with your lips, and do not adhere to him with your hearts? And how do ye fulfil that which followeth: "Behold I send you forth as sheep in the midst of wolves?" Whereas you act quite contrariwise, and proceed as wolves against a flock of sheep: or the other following sentence: "Be ye wise as serpents and simple as doves?" since ye are only wise to bite others with your deadly mouths, and not, with the interposition of your whole body, to defend your head, which is Christ, whom with all the endeavours of your evil actions you tread under foot; neither yet have ye the simplicity of doves, but the resemblance rather of the black crow, which taking her flight out of the ark, that is, the church of God, and finding the carrion of earthly pleasures, did never with a pure return back thither again. But let us look on the rest. "Fear not," saith he, "them who kill the body, but are not able to slay the soul; but fear him who can overthrow both soul and body in hell." Revolve in your minds which of these ye have performed? And what one of you is not wounded in the very secrets of his heart, by this testimony following, which our Saviour uttereth unto his apostles, of evil prelates, saying, "Do ye suffer them, the blind leaders of the blind, but if the blind be a guide to the blind, both shall fall into the ditch?" But the people doubtless whom ye have governed, or rather beguiled, have just occasion to listen hereunto.

96

Mark ye also the words of our Lord speaking unto his apostles, and to the people, which words likewise (as I hear) ye yourselves are not ashamed to pronounce often in public: "Upon the chair of Moses have the scribes and pharisees sat, observe ye therefore and accomplish all that they shall speak unto you, but do not according to their works. For they only speak, but of themselves do nothing." It is truly to priests a dangerous and superfluous doctrine, which is overclouded with sinful actions. "Woe be unto you, hypocrites, who shut up the kingdom of heaven before men, and neither yourselves enter in, nor yet suffer those that would to enter in. "For ye shall with horrible pains be tormented, not only in respect of your great offences, which ye heap up for punishment in the world to come, but also in regard of those who daily perish through your bad example, whose blood in the day of judgment shall be required at your hands.

Yield ye also diligent attention unto the misery, which the parable setteth before your eyes, that is spoken of the servant, who saith in his heart, "My Lord delayeth his coming," and upon this occasion, perchance, "hath begun to strike his fellow servants, eating and drinking with drunkards. The Lord of the same servant, therefore, saith he, will come on a day when he doth not expect him, and in an hour whereof he is ignorant, and will divide him, away from his holy priests, and will place his portion with the hypocrites (that is, with them who under the presence of priesthood do conceal much iniquity), affirming that there shall be weeping and gnashing of teeth;" such as they have not experienced in this present life, either for the daily ruin of the children of our holy mother church, or for the desire of the kingdom of heaven.

97

But let us see what Paul, the true scholar of Christ, and master of the Gentiles, who is a mirror of every ecclesiastical doctor, "Even as I am the disciple of Christ," speaketh about a work of such importance in his first epistle on this wise: "Because when they have known God, they have not magnified him as God, or given thanks unto him; but vanished in their own cogitations, and their foolish heart is blinded; affirming themselves to be wise, they are made fools." Although this seemeth to be spoken unto the Gentiles, look into it notwithstanding, because it may conveniently be applied to the priests and people of this age. And after a few words, "Who have changed," saith he, "the truth of God into lying, and have reverenced and served the creature rather than the Creator, who is blessed for ever; therefore hath God given them over unto passions of ignominy." And again, "And even as they have not approved themselves to have God in their knowledge, so God hath yielded them up to a reprobate sense, that they may do such things as are not convenient, being replenished with all iniquity, malice, uncleanness of life, fornication, covetousness, naughtiness, full of envy murder (i.e. of the souls of the people), contention, deceit, wickedness, backbiters, detractors, hateful to God, spiteful, proud, puffed up, devisers of mischief, disobedient to their parents, senseless, disordered, without mercy, without affection, who, when they had known the justice of God, understood not that they who commit such things, are worthy of death.

98

And now what one of the aforesaid sort hath indeed been void of all these? And if he were, yet perhaps he may be caught in the sense of the ensuing sentence, wherein he saith: "Not only those who do these things, but those also who consent unto them," for none of them truly are free from this wickedness. And afterwards, "But thou, according to thy hardness and impenitent heart, cost lay up for thyself wrath, against the day of wrath, and revelation of the just judgment of God, who will yield unto every one according unto his works." And again, "For there is no acceptation of persons with God. For whosoever have offended without the law, shall also without the law perish; whosoever have offended in the law, shall by the law be judged. For the hearers of the law shall not with God be accounted just, but the doers of the law shall be justified." How severe a sentence shall they therefore sustain, who not only leave undone what they ought to accomplish, and forbear not what they are forbidden, but also flee away from the very hearing of the word of God, as from a serpent, though lightly sounding in their ears.

99

But let us pass over to that which followeth to this effect: "What shall we therefore say, shall we continue still in sin that grace may abound? God forbid, for we who are dead to sin, how shall we again live in the same?" And somewhat afterwards, "Who shall separate us," saith he, "from the love of Christ, tribulation, or distress, or persecution, or famine, or nakedness, or danger, or the sword?" What one, I pray you, of all you, shall with such an affection be possessed in the inward secret of his heart, since ye do not only labour for achieving of piety, but also endure many things for the working of impiety, and offending of Christ? Or who hath respected this that followeth? "The night hath passed, and the day approached. Let us therefore cast off the works of darkness, and put on the armour of light, even as in the day: let us honestly walk, not in banqueting, and drunkenness, not in couches, and wantonness, not in contention, and emulation; but put ye on our Lord Jesus Christ, and make no care to bestow your flesh in concupiscences."

100

And again, in the first Epistle to the Corinthians, he saith: "As a wise workmaster have I laid the foundation, another buildeth thereupon, but let every man consider how he buildeth thereon. For no other man can lay any other foundation besides that which is laid, even Christ Jesus. But if any man buildeth upon this, gold, and silver, precious stones, hay, wood, stubble, every one's work shall be manifest; for the day of our Lord shall declare the same, because it shall be revealed in fire, and the fire shall prove what every man's work is. If any man's work shall remain, all by the fire shall be adjudged. Whoso shall build thereupon, shall receive reward. If any man's work shall burn, he shall suffer detriment. Know ye not that ye are the temple of God, and that the Spirit of God dwelleth in you? But if any man violate the temple of God, God will destroy him." And again, "If any man seemeth to be wise among you in this world, let him be made a fool that he may become wise. For the wisdom of this world is foolishness with God." And within a few words afterwards, "Your glorying is not good. Know ye not that a little leaven corrupteth the whole mass? Purge ye, therefore, the old leaven that ye may be a new sprinkling." How shall the old leaven, which is sin, be purged away, that from day to day with your uttermost endeavours is increased? And yet again, "I have written unto you in mine epistle, that ye be not intermingled with fornicators, not truly the fornicators of this world, or the avaricious, ravenous, or idolatrous, otherwise ye ought to depart out of this world. But now have I written unto you, that ye be not intermingled, if any one is named a brother, and be a fornicator, or avaricious, or an idolator, or a slanderer, or a drunkard, or ravenous, with such an one ye should not so much as eat." But a felon condemneth not his fellow thief for stealing, or other open robbery, whom he rather liketh, defendeth, and loveth, as a companion of his offence.

101

Also in his second epistle unto the Corinthians; "Having therefore," saith he, "this administration, according as we have obtained mercy, let us not fail, but let us cast away the secrets of shame, not walking in subtility, nor yet corrupting the word of God," (that is, by evil example and flattery.) And in that which followeth, he thus discourseth of wicked teachers, saying: "For such false apostles are deceitful workmen, transfiguring themselves into the apostles of Christ. And no wonder: for Satan himself transfigureth himself into an angel of light. It is not much therefore if his ministers are transfigured as ministers of justice, whose end will be according unto their works."

102

Hear likewise what he speaketh unto the Ephesians; and consider if ye find not your consciences attainted as culpable of this that followeth? where he denounceth thus: "I say and testify this in our Lord, that ye do not as now walk like the Gentiles in the vanity of their own sense, having their understanding obscured with darkness, alienated from the way of God, through ignorance, which remaineth in them in regard of the blindness of their heart, who despairing, have yielded themselves over to uncleanness of life, for the working of all filthiness and avarice." And which of ye hath willingly fulfilled that which next ensueth? "Therefore be ye not made unwise, but understanding what is the will of God, and be ye not drunk with wine, wherein there is riotousness, but be ye fulfilled with the Holy Ghost."

103

Or that which he saith to the Thessalonians. "For neither have we been with you at any time in the, speech of flattery, as yourselves do know; neither upon occasion of avarice, neither seeking to be glorified by men, neither by you, nor any others, when we might be honoured, as other apostles of Christ. But we have been made as little ones in the midst of you; or even as the nurse cherisheth her small tender children, so desiring you, we would very gladly deliver unto you, not only the gospel, but also our very lives." If in all things ye retained this affection of the apostle, then might ye be likewise assured, that ye lawfully possessed his chair. Or how have ye observed this that followeth? "Ye know," saith he, "what precepts I have delivered unto you. This is the will of our Lord, your sanctification, that ye abstain from fornication; and that every one of you know how to possess his own vessel, in honour and sanctification, not in the passion of desire, like the Gentiles who are ignorant of God; and that none of you do encroach upon or circumvent his brother in his business, because our Lord is the revenger of all these. For God hath not called us unto uncleanness, but unto sanctification. Therefore whoso despiseth these, doth not despise man, but God." What one also among you hath advisedly and warily kept this that ensueth: "Mortify therefore your members which are upon the earth, fornication, uncleanness of life, lust, and evil concupiscence, for which the wrath of God hath come upon the children of diffidence?" Ye perceive therefore upon what offences the wrath of God doth chiefly arise.

104

In which respect hear likewise what the same holy apostle, with a prophetical spirit, foretelleth of you, and such as yourselves, writing plainly in this sort to Timothy: "For know you this, that in the last days there shall be dangerous times at hand. For men shall be self-lovers, covetous, puffed up, proud, blasphemous, disobedient to their parents, ungrateful, wicked, without affection, incontinent, unmeek, without benignity, betrayers, froward, lofty, rather lovers of sensual pleasures, than of God, having a show of piety, but renouncing the virtue thereof." Avoid thou these men, even as the prophet saith: "I have hated the congregation of the malicious, and with the wicked I will not sit." And a little after, he uttereth that (which in our age we behold to increase), saying: "Ever learning, and never attaining unto the knowledge of truth; for even as Jannes and Mambres resisted Moses, so do these also withstand the truth: men corrupted in mind, reprobate against faith, but they shall prosper no further; for their folly shall be manifest unto all, as theirs likewise was."

105

And evidently doth he also declare how priests in their office ought to behave themselves, writing thus to Titus: "Show thyself an example of good works, in learning, in integrity, in gravity, having thy word sound without offence, that he who standeth on the adverse part may be afraid, having no evil to speak of us." And moreover he saith unto Timothy, "Labour thou as a good soldier of Christ Jesus; no man fighting in God's quarrel entangleth himself in worldly business, that he may please him unto whom he hath approved himself; for whoso striveth in the lists for the mastery, receiveth not the crown, unless he hath lawfully contended." This is his exhortation to the good. Other matter also which the same epistles contain, is a threatening advertisement to the wicked (such as yourselves, in the judgment of all understanding persons, appear to be). "If any one," saith he, "teacheth otherwise, and doth not peaceably assent to the sound sayings of our Lord Jesus Christ, and that doctrine which is according to piety, he is proud, having no knowledge, but languishing about questions, and contentions of words, out of which do spring envies, debates, blasphemies, evil suspicions, conflicts of men corrupted in mind, who are deprived of truth, esteeming commodity to be piety."

106

But why in using these testimonies, here and there dispersed, are we any longer, as it were, tossed up and down in the silly boat of our simple understanding, on the waves of sundry interpretations? We have now therefore at length thought it necessary to have recourse to those lessons, which are gathered out of Holy Scriptures, to the end that they should not only be rehearsed, but also be assenting and assisting unto the benediction, wherewith the hands of priests, and others of inferior sacred orders, are first consecrated, and that thereby they may continually be warned never, by degenerating from their priestly dignity, to digress from the commandments, which are faithfully contained in the same; so as it may be plain and apparent unto all, that everlasting torments are reserved for them, and that they are not priests, or the servants of God, who do not with their utmost power follow and fulfil the instructions and precepts. Wherefore let us hear what the prince of the apostles, Saint Peter, hath signified about this so weighty a matter, saying: "Blessed be God, and the Father of our Lord Jesus Christ, who through his mercy hath regenerated us into the hope of eternal life, by the resurrection of our Lord Jesus Christ from the dead, into an inheritance which can never corrupt, never wither, neither be defiled, preserved in heaven for you, who are kept in the virtue of God;" why then do ye fondly violate such an inheritance, which is not as an earthly one, transitory, but immortal and eternal? And somewhat afterwards: "For which cause be ye girded in the loins of your mind, sober, perfectly hoping in that grace which is offered to you in the revelation of Jesus Christ: "examine ye now the depths of your hearts, whether ye be sober and do perfectly preserve the grace of priesthood, which shall be duly discussed and decided in the revelation of our Lord. And again he saith: "As children of the benediction, not configuring yourselves to those former desires of your ignorance; but according unto him who hath called you holy, be ye also holy in all conversation. For which cause it is written, Be ye holy, because I am holy." Which one of you, I pray, hath with his whole mind so pursued sanctity, that he hath earnestly hastened, as much as in him lay, to fulfil the same? But let us behold what in the second lesson of the same apostle is contained: "My dearest," saith he, "sanctify your souls for the obedience of faith, through the Spirit, in charity, in brotherhood, loving one another out of a true heart perpetually, as born again not of corruptible seed, but of incorruptible, through the word of God, living and remaining for ever."

107

These are truly the commandments of the apostle; and read in the day of your ordination, to the end ye should inviolably observe the same, but they are not fulfilled by you in discretion and judgment, nay not so much as duly considered or understood. And afterwards: "Laying therefore aside all malice, and all deceits, and dissemblings, envy, and detractions, as infants newly born, reasonable and without guile covet ye milk, that ye may thereby grow to salvation, because our Lord is sweet." Consider ye also in your minds, if these sayings which have sounded in your deaf ears have not often likewise been trodden by you under foot: and again: "Ye truly are the chosen lineage, the royal priesthood, tile holy nation, the people for adoption, that ye may declare his virtues who hath called you out of darkness into his marvellous light." But truly by you are not only the virtues of God not declared and made more glorious, but also through your wicked examples are they (by such as have not perfect belief) despised. Ye have perchance at the same time likewise heard, what is read in the lesson of the Acts, on this wise: "Peter arising in the midst of the disciples said: Men and brethren, it is expedient that the Scripture be fulfilled, which the Holy Ghost hath by the mouth of David foretold of Judas." And a little after: "This man therefore purchased a field, of the reward of iniquity." This have ye heard with a careless or rather blockish heart, as though the reading thereof nothing at all appertained unto yourselves. What one of you (I pray you) doth not seek the field of the reward of iniquity? For Judas robbed and pillaged the purse, and ye spoil and waste the sacred gifts and treasures of the church, together with the souls of her children. He went to the Jews to make a market of God, ye pass to the tyrants, and their father the devil, that ye may despise Christ. He set to sale the Saviour of the world for thirty pence, and you do so even for one poor half-penny.

108

What need many words? The example of Matthias is apparently laid before you for your confusion, who was chosen into his place, not by his own proper will, but by the election of the holy apostles, or rather the judgment of Christ, whereat ye being blinded, do not perceive how far ye run astray from his merits, while ye fall wilfully and headlong into the manners and affection of Judas the traitor. It is therefore manifest that he who wittingly from his heart termeth you priests, is not himself a true and worthy Christian. And now I will assuredly speak what I think: this reprehension might have been framed after a milder fashion, but what availeth it to touch only with the hand, or dress with gentle ointment, that wound which with imposthumation or stinking corruption is now grown so horrible, that it requireth the searing iron, or the ordinary help of the fire, if happily by any means it may be cured, the diseased in the meanwhile not seeking a medicine, and the physician much erring from a rightful remedy? O ye enemies of God, and not priests! O ye traders of wickedness, and not bishops! O ye betrayers, and not successors of the holy apostles! O ye adversaries, and not servants of Christ! Ye have certainly heard at the least, the sound of the words, which are in the second lesson taken out of the apostle Saint Paul, although ye have no way observed the admonitions and virtue of them, but even as statues (that neither see nor hear) stood that day at the altar, while both then, and continually since he hath thundered in your ears, saying: "Brethren, it is a faithful speech, and worthy of all acceptance." He called it faithful and worthy, but ye have despised it as unfaithful and unworthy. "If any man desireth a bishopric, he desireth a good work." Ye do mightily covet a bishopric in respect of avarice, but not for spiritual convenience and for the good work which is suitable to the place, ye want it. "It behoveth therefore such a one to be free from all cause of reprehension." At this saying we have more need to shed tears than utter words; for it is as much as if the apostle had said, he ought to be of all others most free from occasion of rebuke. "The husband of one wife," which is likewise so condemned among us, as if that word had never proceeded from him; "Sober, wise;" yea, which of ye hath once desired to have these virtues engrafted in him, "using hospitality." For this, if perchance it hath been found among you, yet being nevertheless rather done to purchase the favour of the people, than to accomplish the commandment, it is of no avail, our Lord and Saviour saying thus: "Verily, I say unto you, they have received their reward." Moreover, "A man adorned, not given to wine; no fighter, but modest; not contentious, not covetous:" O lamentable change! O horrible contempt of the heavenly commandments! And do ye not continually use the force of your words and actions, for the overthrowing or rather overwhelming of these, for whose defence and confirmation, if need had required, ye ought to have suffered pains, yea, and to have lost your very lives.

109

But let us see what followeth: "Well governing," saith he, "his house, having his children subjected with all chastity." Imperfect therefore is the chastity of the parents, if the children be not also endued with the same. But how shall it be, where neither the father, nor the son, depraved by the example of his evil parent, is found to be chaste? "But if any one knoweth not how to rule over his own house, how shall he employ his care over the church of God?" These are the words, that with apparent effects, should be made good and approved. "Deacons in like manner, that they should be chaste, not doubled tongued, not overgiven to much wine, not followers of filthy gain having the mystery of faith in a preconseience, and let these also be first approved, and so let them administer, having no offence." And now trembling truly to make any longer stay on these matters, I can for a conclusion affirm one thing certainly, which is, that all these are changed into contrary actions, in so much that clerks (which not without grief of heart, I here confess,) are shameless and deceitful in their speeches, given to drinking, covetous of filthy lucre, having faith (or to say more truly) unfaithfulness in an impure conscience, ministering not upon probation of their good works, but upon foreknowledge of their evil actions, and being thus defiled with innumerable offences, they are notwithstanding admitted unto the holy office; ye have likewise heard on the same day (wherein ye should with far more right and reason have been drawn to prison or punishment, than preferred unto priesthood) when our Lord demanded whom his disciples supposed him to be, how Peter answered, "Thou art Christ, the Son of the living God;" and our Lord in respect of such his confession, said unto him: "Blessed art thou, Simon Bar-jonas, because flesh and blood hath not revealed it unto thee, but my Father who is in heaven." Peter therefore, instructed by God the Father, did rightly confess Christ; but ye being taught by the devil your father, do, with your lewd actions, wickedly deny our Saviour. It is said to the true priest, "Thou art

Peter, and upon this rock will I build my church:" but ye resembled "the foolish man, who hath builded his house upon the sand." And verily it is to be noted, that God joineth not in the workmanship with the unwise, when they build their house upon the deceitful uncertainty of the sands, according unto that saying: "They have made kings unto themselves, and not by me." Similarly that (which followeth) soundeth in like sort, speaking thus: "And the gates of hell (whereby infernal sins are to be understood) shall not prevail." But of your frail and deadly frame, mark what is pronounced: "The floods came, and the winds blew, and dashed upon that house and it fell, and great was the ruin thereof." To Peter and his successors, our Lord doth say, "And I will give unto thee the keys of the kingdom of heaven." But unto you, "I know you not, depart from me all ye workers of iniquity," that being separated with the goats of the left hand, ye may together with them go into eternal fire. It is also promised unto every good priest, "Whatsoever thou shalt loose upon earth, shall be likewise loosed in heaven: and whatsoever thou shalt bind upon earth, shall be in like sort bound in heaven." But how shall ye loose any thing, that it may be loosed also in heaven, since yourselves for your sins are severed from heaven, and hampered in the bands of your own heinous offences, as Solomon saith, "With the cords of his sins, every one is tied?" And with what reason shall ye bind any thing on this earth, that above this world may be likewise bound, unless it be your only selves, who, entangled in your iniquities, are so detained on this earth, that ye cannot ascend into heaven, but without your conversion unto our Lord in this life, will fall down into the miserable prison of hell?

110

Neither yet let any priest flatter himself upon the knowledge of the particular cleanness of his own body, since their souls (over whom he hath government) shall in the day of judgment be required at his hands as the murderer of them, if any through his ignorance, sloth, or fawning adulation, have perished, because the stroke of death is not less terrible, that is given by a good man, than that which is inflicted by an evil person; otherwise would the apostle never have said that which he left unto his successors, as a fatherly legacy, "I am clear and clean from the blood of all: for I have not forborne to declare unto you all the counsel of God." Being therefore mightily drunken with the use and custom of sins, and extremely overwhelmed with the waves (as it were) of increasing offences, seek ye now forthwith the uttermost endeavours of your minds (after this your shipwreck), that one plank of repentance which is left, whereby ye may escape and swim to the land of the living, that from you may be turned away the wrath of our Lord, who saith, "I will not the death of a sinner: but that he may be converted and live." And may the same Almighty God, of all consolation and mercy, preserve his few good pastors from all evil, and (the common enemy being overcome) make them free inhabitants of the heavenly city of Jerusalem, which is the congregation of all saints; grant this, O Father, Son, and Holy Ghost, to whom be honour and glory, world without end. Amen.

FOOTNOTES:

1) *Notwithstanding this remark of Gildas, the Britons must have shown great bravery and resolution in their battles against the Saxons, or they would not have resisted their encroachments so Long. When Gildas was writing, a hundred years had elapsed, and The Britons still possessed a large portion of their native country.*

2) *Or Aetius*

3) *The description of Britain is given in very nearly the same terms, by Orosius, Bede, and others, but the numbers denoting the length and breadth and other dimensions, are different in almost every MS. Copy.*

4) *"Soporem" in some MSS., "saporem" in others; it is difficult from the turgidity and superabundance of the style to determine which is the best meaning.*

5) *Gildas here confuses the modern idea of a tyrant with that of an usurper. The latter is a sense in which Britain was said to be fertile in tyrants, viz. In usurpers of the imperial dignity.*

6) *Possibly Boudica.*

7) *The Britons who fought under Boadicea were anything but "crafty foxes." "Bold lions" is a much more appropriate appellation; they would also have been victorious if they had half the military advantages of the Romans.*

8) *Or Caerleon.*

9) *The meaning of this expression is not known. O'Connor thinks it is the Irish Sea.*

10) *Or Agitius, according to another reading.*

11) *Isaiah 1. 4,5. In most of these quotations there is great verbal variation from the authorised version: the author probably quoted from memory, if not from the Latin version.*

Milton Keynes UK
Ingram Content Group UK Ltd.
UKHW021826071223
433887UK00015B/1198